Blessings,
Vickie Rutland
Proverbs 3:5-6

Trust and Obey

Finding Your Way
Through the Wilderness

Vickie Lofton Rutland

ISBN: 0692271244

ISBN-13: 9780692271247

For my Lord and Savior, Jesus Christ, who still chooses the foolish things of this earth to confound the wise, and the weak things to confound the mighty.

It is doubtful whether we can be
Christian in anything unless we are
Christian in everything.
                              - A. W. Tozer

Introduction

You shall not take the name of the Lord your God in vain, for the Lord will not hold him guiltless who takes His name in vain. (Exodus 20:7)

I once heard a man who was reared in an Orthodox Jewish home teach on this commandment. His explanation was deeper than anything I had heard before. Modern translations tend to represent only one layer of the meaning. This may reflect an inadequate understanding of the Hebrew language, or perhaps the English language is just too vague to paint as rich a picture as the original Hebrew.

The Hebrew word from which take was translated is Nasa' which means to lift or carry. The word from which name was translated is Shem which means reputation, fame or glory. The word from which vain was translated is Shev', which means emptiness or falsehood. The teacher's translation of the verse was essentially, "You shall not carry the reputation of the Lord your God falsely or aimlessly.

What do our lives tell the world about Jesus? Do we display an authentic picture of the Savior? How do we carry His reputation?

I wonder how many Christians ever stop to consider how closely the world is watching us. The lost want to know whether our faith is real, whether He is real. They need to see that following Christ does make a difference in the life of a believer, both in the way we manage the mundane, and even more so in the way we react when crisis or tragedy strikes.

This reality was brought home to me one evening at the hospital where my sister, Linda, was taken on the night when she was shot. For two months our other sister, Georgia, and I roamed the halls of Memorial University Medical Center, which is a top-notch medical facility, but I think that the layout may have been the product of a couple of 5-year-olds playing Etch-a-Sketch®.

However confusing the landscape, the people who work there, from the maintenance staff to the vendors to the medical staff, and all the way up the chain of management were kind, helpful, and compassionate. They showed great concern both for the emotional and physical needs of their patients as well as for the family members of their patients.

Very long days were divided between waiting for the next ICU visiting hours to roll around and trying to find our way around the hospital. I don't know whether anyone was actually monitoring the feed from all those security cameras in the halls, but I still kind of expect to see the two of us on

YouTube or somewhere as "the two lost ladies with the cart". But we can't fault them for laughing at us; we were laughing at us, too.

Our extended family is very large, very southern, and generally very faithful to Christ. Both of my parents came from large families, and I was blessed with almost forty first cousins, not counting their spouses, many of whom are as close as if they had been born into our family. There were few days when we were not surrounded by loving cousins, some of whom drove upwards of two hours to and from the hospital. They came several times each week, bringing food, hugs, laughter, and encouragement.

In many ways, staying at the hospital was a blessing, almost like a cocoon. There was a certain amount of privacy, providing a layer of insulation from the gossip, daily front-page news reports, and the incessant rumor-mills which operate almost malignantly in small towns everywhere, and especially here in the Deep South.

I was sitting alone in the lobby coffee shop one evening. I remember it as being very late, but it might just as easily have been only about 7 pm; you lose all sense of time in a hospital. As I sipped my herbal tea I was approached by one of the volunteers without whom life would be much harder for the family members of hospital patients. Like everyone else who worked there, she was kind and gracious.

On that evening she stopped by and asked how everyone was doing, and whether we needed anything. We talked for a few minutes and she started to walk away, but stopped. It had not occurred to me that the people whom we regularly encountered had figured out that we were part of that family, the one in the morning headlines. She told me that everyone was impressed with our conduct. They commented on our humility, our kindness to others, our compassion, our undemanding attitudes, and our gratitude for the small things that were done for us.

I guess the people who work at hospitals, especially those with Trauma Units, see all kinds of reactions to crisis. But it is so very sad to realize that we live in a world where humility, compassion and common courtesy are viewed as extraordinary behavior. Yes, our situation was extreme, but the depth of our distress in no way diminished anyone else's suffering. I assured her that it was Christ living through us that they were seeing, certainly nothing special about us, and thanked her for her kindness to us.

That the people we passed in the hall never saw the anger and despair that roiled just beneath the surface of my heart is testimony to the power of The Comforter, the Person of the Holy Spirit. That we were able to laugh more often than cry is testimony of the Joy of the Lord. That we were able to lie down and actually sleep is testimony of His peace that passes understanding.

It was both a privilege and a blessing to be able to pray with and encourage the other hurting people we encountered in waiting rooms and hallways. When we read headlines of violent acts and fatal accidents, it's very easy to forget that these are life stories of real people, real families who are being pulled and tossed by the currents of suffering, fear, and loss. Nowadays, every headline and siren bring me to a moment of prayer for those who are involved in that situation, victims and perpetrators alike.

Prayer is such a powerful weapon in the believer's arsenal. I was, and always will be, thankful for all the people who prayed for us during those hard days. It was only by the grace of the living God that we were able to carry His reputation honorably. These devotions share a little bit of what He taught me in the process.

Entrust the past to God's mercy, the present to His love, and the future to His providence.

-St. Augustine

Part One

When we walk with the Lord
In the light of His Word,
What a glory He sheds on our way;
while we do His good will,
He abides with us still,
And with all who will trust and obey.

For God so loved the world that He gave His one and only Son, that whosoever believes in Him shall not perish, but have eternal life. For God did not send His Son into the world to condemn the world, but to save the world through Him. (John 3:16-17)

We recently collected one of our grandsons from a military base where he had been visiting. As we were leaving the base he asked whether we had military ID cards like the people he was staying with do. I explained that we just get a pass from the gate when we come to visit since we are not in the military.

Curious about the process, he wondered whether we could just buy an ID card. I explained that the ID cards are issued to members of the military when they enlist, there is no other way to get them. Either you are in the military or you are not, based on whether you choose to be. The ID card is given to you by the government as proof that you are part of the military.

Salvation is kind of like that. It is an act of God, not a commodity that we receive. Salvation begins when, by grace, God issues an invitation and endows the invited with enough faith to respond. Those who exercise that faith and accept the invitation enter into an eternal, unbreakable, intimate, love relationship with Majesty. I do not deserve it. There is nothing I can do to earn it. My only part in Salvation is to surrender irrevocably to the safety of His dominion.

If salvation were a commodity given to me to possess, I would surely be in constant danger of losing it. Salvation is a momentary and eternal process of regeneration, by which one who is dead in sin is recreated as one who is alive in Christ. At that moment, I am a new creation, an adopted child of God, as saved as I ever will be. *'I give them eternal life and they shall never perish; no one can snatch them out of my hand. My Father, who has given them to me, is greater than all; no one can snatch them out of my Father's hand. I and the Father are one'. (John 10:28-30)*

But that does not mean that God is finished with me. I am changed just as a soldier, sailor, or airman goes through a training process whereby old habits are broken down while appearance and behavior are reshaped until he conforms to the image of a soldier.

Likewise, the remainder of my earthly life is spent in the process of sanctification whereby every area of my life is remade into the image of Christ, so that I gradually begin to look and behave like the new creature that I have become. The process is a lot slower for some people than for others, but that does not mean that it is not happening.

The Truth is that God is complete within Himself; He doesn't need me or anyone else. But I need God; and Jesus is the only Way to God. It is only through Jesus that I can enter into a relationship with God. Christ's sacrificial death paid the price for my sin and made me righteous before God, *being found in Him, not having a righteousness of my own that comes from the law, but that which is through faith in Christ - the righteousness that comes from God and is by faith. (Philippians 3:9).*

You and I deserve Hell. *But, you see, at just the right time, when we were still powerless, Christ died for the ungodly. Very rarely will anyone die for a righteous man, though for a good man someone might possibly dare to die. But God demonstrates His own love for us in this: While we were still sinners, Christ died for us. (Romans 5:6-8).*

The Word teaches that salvation belongs to God. He lovingly drew me into intimate relationship with Himself; and He keeps the relationship intact through all of eternity. The same grace that caused God to establish the relationship also sealed it. *Now it is God who makes both us and you stand firm in Christ. He anointed us, set His seal of ownership on us, and put His Spirit in our hearts as a deposit, guaranteeing what is to come.(2 Corinthians 1:21-22)*

Salvation is not automatic, nor do you inherit it from your parents, but is freely offered to each person individually. *Whoever believes in Him is not condemned, but whoever does not believe stands condemned already because he has not believed in the name of God's one and only Son. (John 3:18).*

God drew near to be with you and me, so that we can eternally be with Him. While He desires and provided for our eternity, He will not force anyone to accept eternity in His presence any more than He forces them to accept His presence in their earthly lives. Those who reject Him on earth have also rejected Him for all eternity. They choose to send themselves to hell; it is not God's decision, He simply respects the decision they have made for themselves.

God knows us intimately and wants us to know Him. It is true. Jehovah, Adonai, Elohim, however you say His name, He is the LORD my God - the creator of everything. He knows everything that I've ever thought, said, or done and He loves me nonetheless. This isn't a distant or sterile love. It is fierce, active, alive and constantly at work on my behalf.

It is earthshaking and life changing. He knows the truth about me and still wants an intimate, loving, daily and eternal relationship with me.

But because of His great love for us, God, who is rich in mercy, made us alive with Christ even when we were dead in transgressions... For it is by grace you have been saved, through faith - and this not from yourselves, it is the gift of God. (Ephesians 2:4-5, 9)

4

For I am convinced that neither death nor life, neither angels nor demons, neither the present nor the future, nor any powers, neither height nor depth, nor anything else in all creation, will be able to separate us from the love of God that is in Christ Jesus. (Romans 8:38-39)

Growing up in church I memorized John 3:16 at a fairly young age, and I think I became too familiar with the words. Kids usually recite it in a sing-song fashion that often causes them to miss the fire and passion contained in those words.

For God so loved the world... - God has been an active participant in human history ever since He breathed life into Adam's body and the human race began. He lives every moment in relationship with His creation. He does not love the 'world' as a planet full of people. He loves each one of us personally and individually. "*I have loved you with an everlasting love.*" (Jeremiah 31:3)

...that He gave His one and only Son... - He gave Himself. I have four sons and it hurts me so much when they hurt that I cannot imagine loving anyone else enough to allow one of my children to suffer his punishment. But God gave His one and only Son to suffer the punishment for each of our sins.

...that whoever believes in Him... - He desires a relationship with each and every one of us. The invitation is open to all. He loves you just as you are. *But God demonstrates His own love for us in this: While we were still sinners Christ died for us. (Romans 5:8).* Jesus died for you before you were born, and knowing full well every sin you would ever commit.

...shall not perish but have eternal life. - That is so huge, yet so easy to miss. Without Christ you will perish eternally. His sacrifice on the cross is the only acceptable payment for your sin and mine.

God does not need outside relationships. He does not need servants. He is God, He does not need anything. He is complete within Himself. He is able to do whatever He chooses. He can make people out of dirt. He does not need us. However He chose to create us, to love us, to save us, and to give us purpose.

If you don't know Him, please take the time right now to find the peace with God that only Jesus can give.

Simple steps to a relationship with God:

Acknowledge that you are a sinner in need of a Savior. *...for all have sinned and fall short of the glory of God. (Romans 3:23) The wages of sin is death; but the gift of God is eternal life in Christ Jesus our Lord. (Romans 6:23)* Sin merits a spiritual death sentence (eternal judgment).

Trust and Obey

If you confess with your mouth, 'Jesus is Lord,' and believe in your heart that God raised Him from the dead, you will be saved. For it is with your heart that you believe and are justified, and it is with your mouth that you confess and are saved. (Romans 10:9-10). The things we believe in our hearts are the things to which we make a commitment. "To believe in your heart" is to trust in the perfect sacrifice of the resurrected Christ, and surrender to who He is and what He has done. If your believe that Jesus is who He says He is and that He did what His Word says He did, why would you not commit fully to Him?

Pray a simple prayer. Just tell God what is on your heart: "Dear God, I know now that I am a sinner. I am sorry for my sins and want to be a different person than I have been. I believe that Jesus is your Son and that He died in my place. I believe that He rose from the dead and is alive today. I now surrender myself to be His forevermore. I thank you that because of your grace, it is done. I pray this in Jesus' name. Amen."

If you prayed this prayer (or one like it), congratulations on having the wisdom to make the most important decision of your life. Please tell someone about your decision. Either contact me (vlrutland@gmail.com) or some other Believer so that we can celebrate with you, just as Heaven is celebrating. *I tell you there is rejoicing in the presence of the angels of God over one sinner who repents. (Luke 15:10)*

If you are not currently involved in a local church, find one where God's Word is honored and faithfully taught, and get involved. The best way to grow in your relationship with Christ is to spend time with Him each day through prayer and Bible study, and with other Believers. I always recommend that new believers begin with the Gospel of John. It was written for the purpose of increasing faith. After John, I recommend James, which is about the best primer on following Christ that has ever been written. And know that I have prayed for you, and for everyone who will one day read this book, and will continue to do so. I do not yet know your name, but Jesus has known you, and loved you, since the world was spun into orbit.

And so it was, that, while they were there, the days were accomplished that she should be delivered. And she brought forth her firstborn son, and wrapped him in swaddling clothes, and laid him in a manger; because there was no room for them in the inn. (Luke 2:6-7)

There are few things as lovely as a December sky, lit only by the stars. The silent expanse of black velvet sprinkled with the purity of starlight reminds me of the vastness of God's creation, and at the same time surrounds me like eternity itself - encircling but untouchable.

Since we live "out in the country" there are no street lights and it is possible to stand in our yard and see no other light than the stars. I recall a night many Christmases ago when I stood in another rural yard, in another southern state, enthralled by the magnitude of the universe, awestruck by the beauty and wonder of the stars in the winter sky. But when I walked in my door, I was stopped dead in my tracks by the sight of the tiny infant sleeping peacefully in his car seat, my little December baby, Nathaniel.

What moved me so was that the One who created the stars and carefully arranged them in space had made the seemingly absurd decision to enter His creation in the delicate frame of an infant. He had chosen to become entirely dependent upon the provision of those who had disregarded His loving provision, and so fully embraced rebellion that there seemed no remedy for the breach.

When I remember how hard it was for me to leave my children in the care of anyone else, I can only imagine how painful the separation must have been for God. Joseph must have been a remarkable man to have been entrusted with the care and protection of God's only child and His mother.

I cannot grasp a love that would compel God the Father to send His precious Son in such a fragile parcel. How was He able to confine Himself to interact with His eternal companion as if God the Son were a mere creature living in the world that He, Himself had created? I wonder whether there was ever a moment when Father or Son questioned the advisability of allowing the Son to relate to His Father in a completely human way - with free will to choose whether to be faithful to the relationship, or to go the way of Lucifer and Adam.

There was a mutual confidence in their relationship that was born of God the Father's faithfulness, and His power to guarantee that the relationship would remain intact. In the same way, He assures me that He is my God and I am His child.

Today, and every day, may you be overcome by the miracle that is Christmas.

For unto us a child is born, to us a son is given, and the government will be on his shoulders. And he will be called Wonderful Counselor, Mighty God, Everlasting Father, Prince of Peace. Of the greatness of his government and peace there will be no end.... (Isaiah 9:6-7)

The Lord is not slow in keeping his promise, as some understand slowness. Instead he is patient with you, not wanting anyone to perish, but everyone to come to repentance. (2 Peter 3:9)

We have heard it said that someone is as old as Methuselah. But according to scripture (Genesis 5:27), Methuselah actually lived for 969 years. His is the longest lifespan ever recorded. Ironically, he actually died before his father, Enoch, whom the Bible says, *...walked faithfully with God; then he was no more, because God took him away.*

Enoch was the first in a line of four generations of preachers and prophets. Followed by his son Methuselah, grandson Lamech, and great-grandson Noah, their lives represent roughly 1,000 years of warning people of the coming wrath of God - and of their need for repentance.

Indeed, even Methuselah's name foreshadows the coming cataclysm. It comes from two Hebrew roots: muth, which means death; and shalach, which means to bring or send forth. When put together, the name Methuselah means "his death will bring", or "when he dies, it will come." Bible scholars agree that the "it" refers to The Great Flood.

The genealogical record in Genesis 5 reveals that Noah was born when Methuselah was 369; and the flood occurred when Noah was 600 years old, making Methuselah 969 years old when the flood began. Some scholars believe that Methuselah died on the very day that the flood began; others think it was within a few days or weeks. Either way his death was during the same year as the flood and at some point before it began.

In God's great mercy He withheld judgment for an entire millennium to allow many to repent and be saved. But, the people of the Noah's day treated God with contempt and Noah's message with scorn and derision. In the end only eight people, the members of Noah's immediate family, were saved.

Our culture mirrors the world of Noah's day. God, His Son, His Word, His Spirit, and His followers are treated with contempt. Even nominal Christians live as if He doesn't exist. Yet in His mercy He paid the price for our sin, rather than pouring out the wrath that we so richly deserve.

I cannot count the times He has intervened in my own life with mercy rather than the judgment I deserved. He has delivered me from sins, lifted me out of pits, protected me from enemies, curbed consequences, and poured out countless blessings on me, when I deserved the full weight of His wrath.

I sometimes wonder whether there might be another Methuselah alive somewhere on earth right now. Could there be someone out there whose lifespan is the calendar on which God has written the date that even Jesus was not told? Someday Jesus will come back for His Bride, touching off the events that will lead to the final judgment.

I believe it's time for every member of the body of Christ to become as bold in sharing the truth of the Gospel as Noah was in his day. God does not desire that anyone would fall under His wrath, but many will choose to do exactly that. It is vital that those who know the Truth will proclaim it - boldly, lovingly, and respectfully - regardless of how it is received. As Paul wrote,

Pray also for me, that whenever I speak, words may be given me so that I will fearlessly make known the mystery of the gospel, for which I am an ambassador in chains. Pray that I may declare it fearlessly, as I should. (Ephesians 6:19-20)

To the angel of the church in Laodicea write: These are the words of the Amen, the faithful and true witness, the ruler of God's creation. I know your deeds, that you are neither cold nor hot. I wish you were either one or the other! So, because you are lukewarm—neither hot nor cold—I am about to spit you out of my mouth. You say, 'I am rich; I have acquired wealth and do not need a thing.' But you do not realize that you are wretched, pitiful, poor, blind and naked.... Those whom I love I rebuke and discipline. So be earnest and repent. Here I am! I stand at the door and knock. If anyone hears my voice and opens the door, I will come in and eat with that person, and they with me. (Revelation 3:14-20)

The ancient city of Laodicea was located at the intersection of two major trade routes, bringing prosperity and the finest treasures from Asia and Europe to their doorsteps. They were leaders in banking, agriculture, and the manufacture of textiles. There was even a prominent medical and pharmaceutical school located there. Laodicea was among the wealthiest and most cosmopolitan cities of their day. Sounds quite a bit like contemporary America.

As it did in First-Century Laodicea, the stain of materialism has permeated 21st-century America, even capturing the heart of the church. The more things we possess the greater the danger that priorities will shift and our things will begin to possess us. The more activities that occupy our time the greater the likelihood that when we begin to truly understand God's plan for us, the greater will be our regret over the wasted years, even decades, of the precious little time allotted to us on earth.

We think we are doing well, and compared to most of the world we are very wealthy, and are usually the first on the scene to provide aid when there is a natural disaster. We send food and financial assistance around the world, often to our detriment.

But, for all our wealth and good deeds, does God see us as wretched, poor, blind, and naked? Do we even come close to the plan He had for this nation when He inspired our forefathers to embark on this grand experiment? We need only look at the sin and depravity that our culture has redefined as lifestyle choices to answer that question.

Just as was true in ancient Laodicea, God is no longer honored here. I believe He is employing some Divine discipline on us by way of the economic and social woes that plague our nation.

As always, when God's people turn away from Him, He not only has provided the way back, but He also comes to us, mercifully knocking on the doors of lukewarm hearts, waiting for them to be opened.

Warner Sallman was a commercial artist who is best known for some of his Christian images. I'm sure most of the western world is familiar with his portrait, The Head of Christ, which was even distributed to troops by the USO during WWII. Another famous Sallman image is, Christ at Heart's Door. To me, the most striking thing about it is that there is no hardware on Christ's side of the door. Like the door to each of our hearts, it must be opened from the inside.

All too often we want to keep Jesus just outside the door so that we can open the door and grab what we want from Him without having to surrender any territory to His Lordship. We have it upside down. He is God. But He does not exist to serve us. He already has done far more for us than we deserve. In Christ, victory comes only through surrender.

To the one who is victorious, I will give the right to sit with me on my throne, just as I was victorious and sat down with my Father on his throne. Whoever has ears, let them hear what the Spirit says to the churches. (Revelation 3:21-22)

Beloved, do not believe every spirit, but test the spirits to see whether they are from God, for many false prophets have gone out into the world. By this you know the Spirit of God: every spirit that confesses that Jesus Christ has come in the flesh is from God, and every spirit that does not confess Jesus is not from God. This is the spirit of the antichrist, which you heard was coming and now is in the world already. Little children, you are from God and have overcome them, for He who is in you is greater than He who is in the world. They are from the world; therefore they speak from the world, and the world listens to them. We are from God. Whoever knows God listens to us; whoever is not from God does not listen to us. By this we know the Spirit of truth and the spirit of error. (1 John 4:1-6)

*W*hat is truth? Even before Pontius Pilate posed that question on that fateful Friday some 2000 years ago, philosophers debated the possibility of absolute truth within the realm of practical thought. Sadly, society has succumbed to the lie that there is no absolute truth; everything is relative, or perhaps subjective. Armed only with human wisdom man has floundered in the shallow waters of humanistic philosophy ever since the serpent approached Adam and Eve in the Garden.

Whether it's Universalism, Relativism, Existentialism, Humanism, Hinduism, Buddhism, Islamism, or Pseudo-Christian cults - all philosophical world views and works-based religions eventually either self-destruct on the sword of human frailty, or else degenerate into chaos. It is not possible to achieve perfection while we dwell in a fallen body in an imperfect world.

Christianity stands alone on the grace of God and the atoning death of Jesus Christ for bringing trustworthy answers to the uncertainty that faces humanity in the darkness that shrouds our culture.

The false prophets of which John wrote increasingly fill the pulpits in Christian churches. They preach a false gospel of entitlement founded on mercy without repentance, prosperity without sacrifice, success without discipline, happiness without obedience. They own private jets, television networks, and draw in crowds by the thousands, all the while assuring their hapless followers that if they sow into the ministry they will reap great wealth.

They peddle their gospel of social psychology with religious undertones from the pulpit and in millions of books. Their influence is miles wide and about a scintilla deep.

John continues: *God is light; in Him there is no darkness at all. If we claim to have fellowship with Him and yet walk in the darkness, we lie and do not live out the truth.*

13

But if we walk in the light, as He is in the light, we have fellowship with one another and the blood of Jesus, His Son, purifies us from all sin. If we claim to be without sin, we deceive ourselves and the truth is not in us. If we confess our sins, He is faithful and just and will forgive us our sins and purify us from all unrighteousness. If we claim we have not sinned, we make Him out to be a liar and His word is not in us. (1 John 1:5-10)

The counseling ministry where I volunteer provides me the opportunity to deal with young women whose lives are often fiascoes. The client's relationship with God is usually the best place to start in determining the direction we need to go to find workable solutions to their problems. The clients who claim to have a "good" relationship with God almost invariably listen to, and use devotional materials from one such pastor.

They sit comfortably under his teaching while living immoral lives, making mistake after mistake. They see nothing wrong with their lives even though they are in desperate situations. They have little understanding of the concept of sin, much less the consequences.

Those within the Body of Christ who thoughtlessly watch these programs and buy the books are participating in the destruction of generations to come. We owe it to our children and grandchildren to use Spirit-led discernment and call the false prophets to repentance. It is as sinful to treat lies as if they were true as it is to treat Truth as if it is meaningless.

What sets Christianity apart from religion is that Christianity is based on an intimate relationship with a living, personal, active God rather than a set of beliefs. Unlike Mohammad, Buddha, Shiva et al, Jesus Christ is alive and actively involved in the lives of those who serve Him.

In religion success is performance-based requiring its followers to perform deeds, keep rituals, etc. in order to earn a final reward or punishment. Everything depends on human effort to please or appease a physically and relationally distant deity. Success is achieved if you are able to tip the scales by doing more good than bad, as defined by whichever belief system is followed.

But in Jesus Christ, we find GRACE: God's Redemption At Christ's Expense. Grace paid the price for the forgiveness of my debt of sin. In my mind's eye, I can see a scale weighed down with the guilt of my sin. Even now I can feel the hopelessness that first brought me to the foot of the cross.

It is an admittedly imperfect analogy, but much like the process of declaring bankruptcy, you have a choice to make. Bankruptcy relief was originally established in the days when debtor's prison was the norm. It was developed to provide relief in extreme situations where someone found themselves overwhelmed by debts that, due to circumstances beyond their control, they were unable to repay.

I am not a lawyer so this is definitely not meant to be legal advice. But as I understand it, in the United States, individuals can declare either Chapter 7 or Chapter 13 Bankruptcy. Debt never just disappears. In both systems someone must pay; the difference between them is who pays.

Chapter 13 Bankruptcy is much like works-based religions. You must pay some or all of the debt. The debtor holds onto his assets and the court defines a repayment schedule for you to, in a sense, "work off your debt". If you fulfill all the requirements of repayment and reorganization, eventually your debt is discharged.

But in Chapter 7, you surrender all your assets to the court for disposal according to the wisdom of the court, and the debt is forgiven in full. Notice I didn't say that the debt goes away. Your creditors suffer the loss.

The reason this is an imperfect analogy is that it isn't possible to truly pay your sin-debt by human effort. God is perfect in Holiness and Righteousness, and His standard is perfection. But since perfection is humanly impossible, He paid the price to secure our forgiveness.

Just as the petitioners in a bankruptcy case stand before a judge, there is a day of judgment coming for us. *As surely as I live, says the Lord, every knee will bow before me; every tongue will confess to God. (Romans 4:11)*

Every knee will bow and every tongue confess - but will it be in joy as you are welcomed into heaven? Or will you face an eternity of grief, confusion, and terror as you realize that the lies you believed in your rebellion were just that - self-deception.

There is absolute Truth and He can be known. His name is Jesus Christ. He died to pay your sin debt and mine in full. His scars are proof that the debt is paid. We need only to trust in the reality of Who He is and what He has done. Out of this belief will flow a life of obedience born of gratitude for His mercy, not from a vain attempt to even the scales.

Therefore, there is now no condemnation for those who are in Christ Jesus, because through Christ Jesus the law of the Spirit of life set me free from the law of sin and death. (Romans 8:1-2)

Like it or not, we are leading the next generation. If we fail to teach them the difference between truth and lies, we will surely lead them astray.

If you hold to my teaching, you are really my disciples. Then you will know the truth and the truth will make you free. (John 8:31-32)

As I ponder freedom over the days leading up to July 4th, when the USA celebrates our Independence Day, I am struck by how rapidly my freedom to worship as a follower of Christ is eroding. From Christopher Columbus to the Pilgrims who sailed on the Mayflower, the stated purposes of many of the first Europeans to set foot in North America were: first the advancement of the Gospel of Jesus Christ, and second the freedom to worship Him according to their beliefs. Nowadays both have come under fire in this Nation Under God.

It's not as if Christianity is the only faith that claims exclusive Truth, although it seems to be the only one that is criticized for doing so. Hinduism is often touted as being tolerant and inclusive because they boast so many gods. But they hold staunchly to Karma and reincarnation as absolutes. The blood-baths we watch almost daily throughout the Middle East and South Asia testify to Islam's intolerance of all other belief systems. Many of these wars are fought between different sects within Islam. The one thing that all major world religions seem to have in common is that they teach that Jesus Christ was real, and that He was a great teacher or prophet.

The fact is that all religious belief systems claim absolute truth on some level. Since truth is exclusive by nature, all religions can't be true because they contradict each other. The law of non-contradiction says that two contradictory statements cannot both be true in the same sense. If both are true then neither is false. If neither is false then it is also true to say that both are false. We cannot have it both ways. To deny the law of non-contradiction is to also affirm the law of non-contradiction. So what is true? Or better yet, What is Truth?

Truth is not a what, but a Who. Jesus said, *I am the Way the Truth and the Life. No man comes to the Father except through me. If you really know me, you will know my Father as well. (John 14:6-7)*. In making such a bold and absolute statement, Jesus claimed to be one with God and the only way to God. Either He is exactly who He claimed to be, or He lied. He left us with no middle ground, only a choice. He must either be rejected as a fraud or He must be worshiped as God. As C. S. Lewis wrote in Mere Christianity, "but let us not come with any patronizing nonsense about his being a great human teacher. He has not left that open to us. He did not intend to."

I, for one, am very glad that He left no room for doubt. I want to know that my sins are forgiven and hold no power over my eternal future. I want to live in confidence that when God looks at me He sees, not my sin, but rather the righteousness of Christ.

As John Bunyan put it so beautifully in his book, Grace Abounding, "I thought I saw with the eyes of my soul Jesus Christ at God's right hand. There was my righteousness. Wherever I was, or whatever I was doing, God could not say of me that I lacked his righteousness, for that was ever before Him. Moreover, I saw that it was not my good frame of heart that made my righteousness better, nor my bad frame that made it worse, for my righteousness was Jesus Christ himself."

All too often we build walls of pride, arrogance, greed, or shame between ourselves and God, choosing to believe the enemy's lies that we aren't good enough for God to want us, or that we're too good to need Him, or that there is plenty of time to make a decision later on after we've sinned all we want. But if you fail to choose Him, you choose to reject Him.

What lies are you living for? Do you know The Way, the Truth, and the Life?

In the same way, count yourselves dead to sin but alive to God in Christ Jesus. Therefore do not let sin reign in your mortal body so that you obey its evil desires. Do not offer any part of yourself to sin as an instrument of wickedness, but rather offer yourselves to God as those who have been brought from death to life; and offer every part of yourself to him as an instrument of righteousness. For sin shall no longer be your master, because you are not under the law, but under grace.

What then? Shall we sin because we are not under the law but under grace? By no means! Don't you know that when you offer yourselves to someone as obedient slaves, you are slaves of the one you obey—whether you are slaves to sin, which leads to death, or to obedience, which leads to righteousness? But thanks be to God that, though you used to be slaves to sin, you have come to obey from your heart the pattern of teaching that has now claimed your allegiance. You have been set free from sin and have become slaves to righteousness.

When you were slaves to sin, you were free from the control of righteousness. What benefit did you reap at that time from the things you are now ashamed of? Those things result in death! But now that you have been set free from sin and have become slaves of God, the benefit you reap leads to holiness, and the result is eternal life. For the wages of sin is death, but the gift of God is eternal life in Christ Jesus our Lord. (Romans 6) (Selected verses)

It all started in the Garden when the serpent approached Adam and Eve and asked them, Did God really say? The same question is at the heart of every sin ever committed, and forms the foundation for every false religion in the world.

Today we give sin kinder, gentler names and the words in the Bible no longer seem relevant, therefore the Bible is no longer viewed as significant by much of society. Drunkenness is called alcoholism - sin becomes an illness and beyond the control of the sinner. Apathy becomes tolerance – and sin becomes a virtue. Adultery becomes an affair - sin sounds like a party, a soiree. Greed becomes ambition – somehow part of a good work ethic.

But one of the most disturbing deceptions has been the transformation of witchcraft into child's play - sin becomes a game. In the original Greek text of Galatians 5:19, the word that was translated to witchcraft or sorcery is farmakeia or Pharmakeia which is the use or the administering of drugs; sorcery, magical arts, often found in connection with idolatry and fostered by it. It is the root from which we get the English word pharmacy. How many people today realize that when they are popping pills, snorting, smoking, or shooting up their behavior is as the sin of witchcraft or sorcery (satanic) in God's eyes?

We make Harry Potter-style witchcraft a multi-million dollar business and wonder why sexual immorality and drug abuse are pandemic among ever younger children. There is a dynamic to the occult that we do not fully understand. But the Bible is clear enough that it is nothing to play around with.

When God gave The Ten Commandments to Moses, they became the foundation upon which to build a life of integrity. But we see so little of that quality in the government or business sectors of today's society - and even more troubling, within the Church.

God is the same whether you read the New Testament or the Old Testament. The God who kicked Adam and Eve out of paradise is the same One who sacrificed his precious son to atone for the sins of mankind. He didn't suddenly develop a tolerance for willful sin when Jesus died.

The fact that we are "under grace" rather than "under the law" doesn't mean that God has changed His mind about the Ten Commandments or the nature of sin. If anything, with the dispensation of grace came a stricter application of God's law. Jesus said that hatred has the same impact on our souls as murder and lust as adultery. Moses allowed divorce for many reasons. Jesus allowed divorce only in cases of unrepentant adultery.

Jesus came to bring life and freedom from bondage to sin. He offers righteousness in exchange for guilt and shame. He shed His own blood to prove His love. We have only our obedience to prove our love for Him.

Jesus carried the cross of sacrificial obedience on our behalf for 33 years; then He laid down and died on it. Every act of self-denial, every resistance of temptation, every word aptly spoken was a precursor to His death. Living a life of obedience seems a small token of gratitude for such an extravagant gift of love.

Then He said to them all, "If anyone wants to come with Me, he must take up his cross daily and follow Me". (Luke 9:23)

Trust and Obey

It was just before the Passover festival. Jesus knew that the time had come for Him to leave this world and go to the Father. Having loved His own who were in the world, He loved them to the end. (John 13:1)

Maundy Thursday. The word "Maundy" is taken from the Latin word mandatum, the same word from which we get the English word mandate. Jesus used that final Passover evening to prepare His followers for the events that would unfold over the next days and weeks. And to teach them what would be expected of them. He gave them a glimpse of the suffering they would endure and the path their obedience would follow. The Gospel of John dedicates five chapters, almost a fourth of the entire book, to this one evening.

There is perhaps no greater example of Christ's humility than the act of washing His disciples' feet. One by one, He washed the dirt of the past from the feet that would carry His story into the future. I cannot imagine the feelings that must have overcome Jesus as He knelt and lovingly cleansed the feet that would carry Judas Iscariot on the road to betrayal. His grief must have been almost unbearable.

He knew God's timing is always right, but there must have been more that Jesus wanted to teach these men who had walked with Him those last three years. He crammed a lot into that evening, always pointing them to greater faith in God. Even His prediction of Judas' betrayal and Peter's denial may have offered comfort to the Apostles in the months and years to come when persecution arose as He had predicted.

The very heart of Jesus' ministry on earth was obedience to His Father. Jesus didn't come and die only because He loved us; He did it because He loves God. It was the supreme example of the life that God requires of those who love Him. In His death and resurrection we see that as we lay down our lives, our desires, our rights, our hopes and dreams at His feet - entrusting all to His loving care, just as Jesus did, there is a new and eternal life awaiting us that transcends even physical death.

God is perfect in love and complete within Himself. He does not need us. He simply does not need. But His love is so great that He opens His arms to provide a Way for us into a perfect love relationship with Him.

He didn't promise that the life He calls us to would be easy, that there would be no pain, no sorrows, no storms. But He has promised His Spirit, His peace, comfort, strength, and joy in the midst of all of this world's hardships. And He has proven time and again that nothing will ever be beyond His reach, and that the wind and waves will always obey His voice.

Before He led the eleven out of the upper room, Jesus prayed for them, and for us. He knew us even then. He knew that we would one day live, and that we would need the salvation that only He could secure for us. He knew that the Cross awaited.

When He had finished praying, Jesus left with His disciples and crossed the Kidron Valley. On the other side there was a Garden, and He and his disciples went into it. (John 18:1).

Do not store up for yourselves treasure on earth, where moth and vermin destroy, and where thieves break in and steal. But store up for yourselves treasure in heaven, where moth and vermin do not destroy, and where thieves do not break in and steal. For where your treasure is, there your heart will be also. (Matthew 6:19-21)

There are still places in the world where life is conducted much as it was during the First Century. I recently read the story of a young man who lives in one such place. He attends a Bible School in hopes of becoming a better witness for Christ, but he has to travel about 60 miles each way to get to his school.

The journey takes him more than two days on foot. He has to cross a river and mountains. The area where he lives is so remote that there is no cash economy. His carries his tuition the entire way from home – five live chickens.

How many of us would walk for two days, over river and mountains (even without the live chickens), just to study God's Word? How many of us won't even get up 30 minutes earlier or stay up 30 minutes later to spend time with God, the One who always makes time for us? How many of us won't push the off button on the TV remote or shut down the computer in order to hear from our Creator? How many of us won't even walk across the room to pick up our Bibles? How many of us don't even know where our Bibles are?

One stumbling block to salvation by grace is that we often think that if something is free, it must be of little or no value. The Bride of Christ seems to be suffering from identity crisis. We may have forgotten that we are not involved in a religious organization, but rather a covenant relationship that was sealed in blood.

It is humbling to learn the stories of modern giants of the faith, living passionate lives under the most difficult conditions imaginable. I try to think about this young man and the thousands like him around the world, who face such adversity, when I am tempted to hit the snooze button or spend hours mindlessly scanning the television channels or surfing the net.

How is it that the underprivileged, unimposing people of the developing world treasure His Word so much more than we do? Maybe they just see Him more clearly.

God could have sent His Son at any time of History. He chose an era when there was no mass communication or mass transportation. There was no mass marketing or mass production. Jesus walked almost everywhere He went. He never possessed great earthly wealth.

At the same time, He possessed everything in all creation – Heaven and earth. He had unlimited resources. He knew every language; He understood electricity, physics, aerodynamics and thermodynamics. He inspired the greatest music, art, and poetry ever created. There are legions of angels at His command.

He didn't have to leave His home or come for us. He did not have to do any of it. He could have stayed on His throne.

His priorities were in perfect order. Because His love is perfect, He came in obedience to His Father's will. He lived a life of obedience to fulfill the law. He died in obedience to God's plan to secure eternity for us. He arose victorious to prove to us that His word is true. And He ascended to the right hand of God in His resurrected body, to make intercession for us. How do our priorities measure up?

Greater love has no one than this, that he lay down his life for his friends. *(John 15:13).*

Trust and Obey

The reason my Father loves me is that I lay down my life - only to take it up again. No one takes it from me, but I lay it down of my own accord. I have authority to lay it down and authority to take it up again. This command I received from my Father. (John 10:17-18)

There are some events so sacred, so holy, so inviolable that they must be treated with genuine reverence. Chief among these is the crucifixion of Jesus Christ, which ranks along with the resurrection of Christ as the greatest historical events since the creation. That weekend nearly 2000 years ago made the difference between life and death, darkness and light, hope and despair for all of humanity, for all of time.

Each year during the Easter season believers throughout the world attend programs depicting this holiest moment in all history. I've witnessed some of the most amazing passion plays, cantatas, and dramatic presentations imaginable.

I was privileged to participate in a production entitled The Light, which was written by a wonderfully gifted man of God, named Wayne Johnson; and was presented by the choir, orchestra, and drama group at First Baptist Church of Orlando, Florida. It was such a massive undertaking that Wayne used to say it was "like doing Ben Hur, live". There was no chariot race, but otherwise it came pretty close.

The program began with the annunciation and ended with the second coming of Christ. The entire pulpit area, 500-seat choir loft, and orchestra pit of the Worship Center were transformed each spring into the city of Jerusalem. There were priests at the Temple; slaves, beggars, lepers, prostitutes, tradesmen, shoppers at the marketplace, and Roman soldiers overseeing all of it. There was a stable that was rolled into position for the birth of a tiny baby, a small house that was the home of a humble carpenter and his growing family, a garden, a tomb, and there was a hill.

Over the span of an evening we were transported back in time as a tiny babe became a little boy playing in the street, a 12-year-old in the Temple, a young man teaching, preaching, healing, and raising the dead. We experienced a last supper, a time of agonizing prayer in a garden, and a counterfeit trial in a pagan court.

There were heartbreaking cries as whips tore flesh, and the glorious strains of Via Dolorosa, as a bloodied, but determined man carried a cross piece through the auditorium. We saw him stumble under the weight, and with a conscripted Simon carrying the cross, we watched Him willingly climb that hill. We heard the pounding of hammer to nail. As the cross was lifted up, it wrenched at every part of his body as the base dropped into the hole.

Asphyxiation was the actual cause of death by crucifixion. The actor who portrayed Christ on the cross confirmed that he couldn't breathe in that position, supported only at his hands and feet. It was necessary to push up with the legs in order to fill his lungs. We watched him struggle to breathe, heard him proclaim It is finished, and watched him die.

As darkness fell over the cross, there was thunder, lightning, and an earthquake. They took his limp body down and laid him at the foot of the cross with his head in his mother's lap. It was so realistic and so profound that even after portraying a mourner in 6 or 7 presentations for each of 5 years, my tears were always real.

The event was bathed in prayer, and through the work of the Holy Spirit, hundreds of people came to know Christ each year. Standing there looking up at the crucifixion scene made me so painfully aware of the price that was paid for my sin.

Neither Pilate, the Jewish religious leaders, nor the soldiers took Jesus' life from Him. He didn't have to die. He didn't even have to come to earth in the frail form of a man. He chose to come. He chose to die. I'll never understand why He did that for you and me, but I'm so thankful that He did.

Samuel told all the words of the Lord to the people who were asking him for a king. He said, "This is what the king who will reign over you will claim as his rights: He will take your sons and make them serve with his chariots and horses, and they will run in front of his chariots. ...He will take the best of your fields and vineyards and olive groves and give them to his attendants. He will take a tenth of your grain and of your vintage and give it to his officials and attendants. Your male and female servants and the best of your cattle and donkeys he will take for his own use. He will take a tenth of your flocks, and you yourselves will become his slaves.

When that day comes, you will cry out for relief from the king you have chosen, but the Lord will not answer you in that day." But the people refused to listen to Samuel. "No!" they said. "We want a king over us. Then we will be like all the other nations, with a king to lead us and to go out before us and fight our battles." When Samuel heard all that the people said, he repeated it before the Lord. The Lord answered, "Listen to them and give them a king." (1 Samuel 8:6-21)

Had Samuel followed his instincts in selecting a man to follow Saul's disastrous reign, the nation of Israel would have been doomed. Whenever we have choices to make, it's essential that we seek God's direction as Samuel did when it was time to anoint a new King of Israel.

In choosing relationships it is easy for even the most discerning to be fooled. Only God can see into the human heart. Only He knows the true character of a man. Only He can be trusted to reveal the truth and prevent the travesty experienced by the nation of Israel under Saul, and many nations since.

Many politicians vainly use God's name as a public relations tool in their campaigns for power. But if they aren't committed to God, they are against God. As we have seen of late, their word cannot be trusted; they will surely lead a nation astray.

Those of us who call ourselves followers of Christ, have failed to ask God for direction in the important decisions of our lives. And we've participated in the election of many key leaders who turned out to be very foolish choices indeed. As Christ-followers, shouldn't the principles established by God be the deciding factor in choosing which candidate deserves our votes?

Instead, we read headlines, listen to sound bites, and having no idea what he really believes, we often vote for the most handsome, most charming, or best orator in the field. The result is that we have elected far too many smooth-talking snake-oil salesmen and women with million-dollar smiles and no integrity. We can't afford to be deceived by charm, style, looks, or worldly intellectualism.

Our culture, even the Church, has become possessed by the spirit of Hezekiah who, after a long and God-pleasing reign, became proud and complacent in his old age. When confronted by Isaiah about his sinful attitude, *Then Isaiah said to Hezekiah, "Hear the word of the LORD: the time will surely come when everything in your palace, and all that your predecessors have stored up until this day will be carried off to Babylon. Nothing will be left, says the LORD. And some of your descendants, your own flesh and blood who will be born to you, will be taken away, and they will become eunuchs in the palace of the king of Babylon." (2 Kings 20:16-18).*

"The word of the LORD you have spoken is good", Hezekiah replied. For he thought, "Will there not be peace and security in my lifetime?" (2 Kings 20:19). The future of our children and their children dictates that we should seek God's direction before we enter a voting booth.

As Patrick Henry said in his famous "Give Me Liberty or Give Me Death Speech", "We are apt to shut our eyes against a painful truth, and listen to the song of that siren, till she transforms us into beasts. Is this the part of wise men, engaged in a great and arduous struggle for liberty? Are we disposed to be of the number of those who, having eyes, see not, and having ears, hear not, the things which so nearly concern their temporal salvation?

For my part, whatever anguish of spirit it may cost, I am willing to know the whole truth -- to know the worst and to provide for it."

We must open our eyes to see the direction that we as a nation are headed lest we fulfill Khrushchev's prophecy that socialism (with its accompanying ills of poverty, Godlessness, and oppression) would someday overcome the United States "without firing a shot".

Despite revisionist history, judicial activism, and political intolerance Christians are still part of the political conversation in this nation. The myth that faith has no place in our government is belied by the words of the first Chief Justice of the Supreme court, John Jay: "Providence has given to our people the choice of their rulers, and it is the duty, as well as the privilege and interest of a Christian nation to select and prefer Christians for their rulers." From a letter to Jedidiah Morse dated February 28, 1797.

It is imperative for those in this nation who are called by the name of Christ to pray. We must pray first in repentance of the depravity we have tolerated in silence, and of the apathy or foolishness that has put corrupt leaders in office.

God will only respond to the prayers of the regenerate. The lost have no part in Him. *If my people, who are called by my name, will humble themselves and pray and seek my face and turn from their wicked ways, then I will hear from heaven, and I will forgive their sin and will heal their land. (2 Chronicles 7:14)*

We must pray for wisdom when we enter a voting booth. We must pray for our elected officials to turn their hearts toward the God of the Bible, and honor Him as our forefathers did. We must pray for another Great Awakening to sweep across this nation.

Finally, we must get back to the business of the Church, the spread of the Gospel, so that it will again be true of America that: *The people walking in darkness have seen a great light; on those living in the land of deep darkness a light has dawned. (Isaiah 9:2)*

Just as He did for us individually at the moment of our conversion, God can deliver us collectively from our enemies, and He can deliver us from the sins of our past. This will only happen if we throw off the spirit of Hezekiah and take up the cause of securing the same freedom for generations to come that were bestowed upon us by the blood and faith in God of generations past.

Finally, be strong in the Lord and in the strength of his might. Put on the whole armor of God, that you may be able to stand against the schemes of the devil. For we do not wrestle against flesh and blood, but against the rulers, against the authorities, against the cosmic powers over this present darkness against the spiritual forces of evil in the heavenly places. Therefore take up the whole armor of God, that you may be able to withstand in the evil day, and having done all, to stand firm. (Ephesians 6:10-13

"There is still the youngest." Jesse answered, "He is tending the sheep". (1 Samuel 16:11)

As soon as he saw Eliab, tall, strong, and handsome - likely regal in his bearing, Samuel was certain that he had found God's choice to be the next king of Israel. But, Samuel was wrong. Perhaps Abinadab was the chosen one? No. Shammah? No.

On they came. One by one, Jesse's sons paraded past Samuel; and one by one God rejected them, seven strong, fit, young men. Until finally, Samuel had to ask, Are these all the sons you have? And when only the youngest, 'the runt of the litter', the one allowed only to tend the sheep, when only David was left, God said, ...*He's the one.*

Samuel anointed David who returned to tending the sheep. After a time the anointed king was splitting his time between tending his father's sheep and serving King Saul as armor-bearer. His brothers Eliab, Abinadab, and Shammah were encamped with Saul's army atop a hill overlooking the Valley of Elah. Across the valley, another hill is entrenched with the Philistine army.

Every morning and every evening, for forty days, the valley echoed with the taunts of the Philistine giant, Goliath, almost ten feet tall and bulletproof behind his heavy bronze armor. For forty days and forty nights, King Saul, Eliab, Abinadab, Shammah, and the rest of Israel's army shivered in their sandals as they listened to Goliath's thunderous threats - dismayed and terrified.

One day Jesse sent little David to the battlefield with provisions for his brothers. He was stunned to see the army of God's chosen people skulking in the distance, kept at bay by nothing more than the taunts and insults of a pagan colossus.

Outraged at the cowardice of Israel's army, David asked the men standing near him, ...*Who is this uncircumcised Philistine that he should defy the armies of the living God?*

As is common among brothers, Eliab bristled at little brother David's supposed arrogance and began to belittle him, *Why have you come down here? And with whom did you leave those few sheep in the desert? I know how conceited you are and how wicked your heart is; you came down only to watch the battle.*

David's exasperated response, *Now what have I done? Can't I even speak?* sounds all too familiar to any mother who has been blessed to parent more than one child. The defensiveness often seen in a beleaguered youngest child is almost palpable. But after silencing his big brother, an undeterred David resumed his discussion with the other soldiers.

The exchange was reported to Saul who, after some negotiation, sent David out alone to face Goliath, stopping only to collect five smooth stones from the dry creek bed.

How God must have smiled at David's faith-filled response to Goliath's taunts: *You come against me with sword and spear and javelin. But I come against you in the name of the LORD Almighty, the God of the armies of Israel, whom you have defied. This day the LORD will deliver you into my hands, and I'll strike you down and cut off your head. This very day I will give the carcasses of the Philistine army to the birds and the wild animals, and the whole world will know that there is a God in Israel. All those gathered here will know that it's not by sword or spear that the LORD saves; for the battle is the LORD's and He will give you into our hands."*

And that's exactly what happened. A sling, one smooth stone, a beheaded giant, and the Philistines turned and ran, with the Israeli army in emboldened pursuit.

God knew Eliab lacked both the resolve and the courage to lead a nation. But, God saw what neither Eli, Jesse, nor any of David's brothers could see. David had the heart of a leader. He understood the sovereignty of God. Despite a lot of mistakes, and many sins, David sought to rule the nation of Israel under the authority of God. Unlike King Saul, the people's king, King David was a man after God's own heart.

Saul's reign had been God's judgment on the desire of the Israelite people to replace God's direct rule with an earthly king. It was bowing to peer pressure on a grand scale: But when they said, *Give us a king to lead us,* this displeased Samuel; so he prayed to the Lord. And the Lord told him: *Listen to all that the people are saying to you; it is not you they have rejected, but they have rejected me as their king. As they have done from the day I brought them up out of Egypt until this day, forsaking me and serving other gods, so they are doing to you. Now listen to them; but warn them solemnly and let them know what the king who will reign over them will claim as his rights.*

Now we know that if the earthly tent we live in is destroyed, we have a building from God, an eternal house in heaven, not built by human hands. Meanwhile we groan, longing to be clothed with our heavenly dwelling, because when we are clothed, we will not be found naked. For while we are in this tent, we groan and are burdened, because we do not wish to be unclothed but to be clothed with our heavenly dwelling, so that what is mortal may be swallowed up by life. Now it is God who has made us for this very purpose and has given us the Spirit as a deposit, guaranteeing what is to come.

Therefore, we are confident and know that as long as we are at home in the body we are away from the LORD. For we live by faith not by sight. We are confident, I say, and would prefer to be away from the body and at home with the LORD. So we make it our goal to please Him, whether we are at home in the body or away from it. For we must all appear at the judgment seat of Christ, so that each of us may receive what is due us for the things done while in the body, whether good or bad. (2 Corinthians 5:6-10)

As a child in Sunday School and GA's I memorized the "Great Commission" – Matthew 28:19-20: *Therefore go and make disciples of all nations, baptizing them in the name of the Father and of the son and of the Holy Spirit, and teaching them to obey everything I have commanded you. And surely I am with you always, to the very end of the age.*

That was such an intimidating command in my childish heart, especially since we sort of skipped over the most power-filled word in the verse, "therefore" – which means "consequently" and "these things being so". But to what does the therefore refer? It is such a disservice to teach Matt. 28:19-20 without the foundation of verse 18.

Travel back in time with me to ancient Galilee … Jesus has been crucified and risen again. He has called a staff meeting with the eleven remaining disciples and they are gathered at the appointed place on a mountainside in Galilee. The disciples can hardly believe what they are seeing: Him. There. Alive. Awestruck in the presence of the Living God, despite some lingering doubts, they worshipped Him.

I cannot even imagine how it must have felt to sit face to face with the risen Christ, waiting for Him to speak. Matt 28:17-18 says, *When they saw Him, they worshiped Him; but some doubted. Then Jesus came to them and said, All authority in Heaven and on earth has been given to me. Therefore* (consequently, this being so - the truth that, once fully believed, will lead to the natural consequence of obedience to the command which follows): *go and make disciples.*

We have commissioning services for missionaries before they are sent to harvest foreign fields. But aren't all who belong to the Body of Christ commissioned at the moment of salvation, the moment when we accept His precious gift of atonement for our sin nature. The moment when we surrender our will to His authority

We have the God-given freedom to decide whether or not to accept His gift of salvation. Failure to accept salvation is to accept damnation, that fact cannot be overstated. Those who, by faith, choose to accept His gift of salvation are exchanging their will (ethos, plans, desires, etc.) for God's will. Faith is understanding who Jesus is and submitting to the authority that has been given to Him: All authority in Heaven and on earth.

From the moment of acceptance, we are either submitted His authority or we are in rebellion against His authority. There is no gray area. It is black and white – obedience or rebellion. Either you fall on your knees before Him or, in His timing, He will put you on your knees. A terrifying thought unless you know the character of God. He is Good. All that He does is for our good. Everything. He never harms His children. As Jesus said, *No one is good except God alone. (Mark 10:18)*

I have been disciplined by God more often than I care to remember. But His discipline was always for my good. True discipline is about teaching, not punishment; and God's discipline is evidence of His love.

Those who have been saved by the blood of Christ will never suffer God's wrath. I have, however, suffered the consequences of my wrong thoughts and actions. I have felt the weight of my sins; and I have dealt with the fallout.

But always, after repentance comes restoration and gratitude that He loves me enough to straighten me out when I stray. His discipline always leads to humility, an increase in faith, and a renewed passion for serving Him.

Every interaction with another human being should be a reflection of my relationship with God. As long as I remain aware whose authority governs my life, I will be about the business of making disciples - whether I am interacting with family, friends, or coworkers; or I am serving in some distant land, or just working in the nursery at church. I must be about His business.

*Trust in the Lord with all
your heart and lean not on
your own understanding; in
all your ways submit to
Him and He will make
your paths straight.*

— Proverbs 3:5-6

Part Two

Not a shadow can rise,
Not a cloud in the skies,
But His smile quickly drives it away;
Not a doubt or a fear,
Not a sigh or a tear,
Can abide while we trust and obey.

Consider it pure joy, my brothers, whenever you face trials of many kinds; because you know that the testing of your faith develops perseverance. Perseverance must finish its work so that you may be mature and complete, not lacking anything. If any of you lacks wisdom, he should ask God, Who gives generously to all without finding fault, and it will be given to him. (James 1:2-4)

Trials come in many forms and for many reasons. Sometimes we fall victim to our own sin and bad choices. Other times our trials are the result of someone else's bad choices or deliberate attempts to do us harm. Many times it seems to be just life in a fallen world -- the economy goes bad, natural disasters strike, etc.

Whatever the cause of our trials, one thing is certain. God allows them. He is omnipotent; He could prevent them. Yet He chooses to allow them, but always for a purpose. Always to accomplish His purpose either for our own good or for His glory, usually both.

Faith is a wonderful gift from God. *For it is by grace you have been saved; through faith--and this not of yourselves, it is the gift of God... (Ephesians 2:8)* I believe that God gives us the initial faith to believe and become followers of Christ. I also believe that He uses His Word to galvanize and expand that faith. And I believe that He allows trials and tests in our lives to prove that faith. Our trials bring Him glory by showing the world that He is bigger than any trial. And they build our faith as they prove that His Word is true and wholly trustworthy.

Finding joy in the midst of trials and storms comes not in finding answers and solutions, but in finding the One who provides strength, comfort, faith, hope, and courage to just keep going -- saying with David, *Even though I walk through the valley of the shadow of death, I will fear no evil, for You are with me.... (Psalm 23:4)*

So, whatever valley you are in rejoice in the truth that you are not there alone. If you have been saved by the grace of God, through faith in Christ, you have all the faith you need to get through this trial; and when you reach the other side of this storm, your faith will have grown enough to enable you to persevere through the next one.

As Jesus said, *I have told you these things, so that in Me you may have peace. In this world you will have trouble. But take heart! I have overcome the world. (John 16:33)*

Dear friends, do not be surprised at the fiery ordeal that has come on you to test you, as though something strange were happening to you. But rejoice inasmuch as you participate in the sufferings of Christ, so that you may be overjoyed when His glory is revealed. (1 Peter 4:12-13)

I love flowers. I sometimes am privileged to make table arrangements for the annual banquet to benefit a ministry where I volunteer, or some other social occasion. It's really a lot of fun, and I've learned some fascinating things about flowers. Tulips have joined roses and daisies as favorites of mine.

The thing that makes tulips especially fun is that they continue to grow a little, sometimes as much as an inch each day, even after they've been cut. A vase of tulip blooms becomes an ever-changing sculpture, with the stems winding in sundry directions, providing a lovely surprise each day. Despite the trauma of having been removed from the familiar nourishment of their parent plant, wrapped in a plastic sleeve, thrust into the darkness of a cardboard box, and shipped to some strange land (usually without water), they continue to grow - always in search of light.

Sometimes we find ourselves in strange circumstances, ripped away from those we love and all that is familiar to us, alone in the darkness. Whether we suffer the loss of a loved one, physical sickness or disability, betrayal by those we love and trust, financial ruin, abuse, persecution, or abandonment, it's imperative that we not neglect our relationships with Christ.

Our pain is precious to God. He doesn't enjoy our sufferings, nor is He powerless to remove them. He often permits pain in order to refine our character, renew our minds, and strengthen our faith. It's during the storm that we learn that He can calm storms - or calm His child in the midst of the storm.

As we go through trials we see Him act on our behalf as Comforter, Healer, Faithful Companion, Provider, Protector, Encourager, and Rescuer. I don't think you can fully know Him without undergoing trials.

God is light. He shines His light on us as we seek Him through the study of His Word, through prayer, and through worship. The trials we face can only accomplish His purpose in us if we keep our focus on Him. When everything within us wants to give up and die, we can find victory and joy if we will continue to grow rather than to succumb.

Much like our mortal bodies, problems are temporary. God's promises are eternal. Peace and joy are eternal. My family has endured trials and

37

suffering that few can imagine. I would be lying if I said I wouldn't want to change some things that have happened to the people I love.

But, in the midst of tremendous suffering, I've also seen tremendous miracles. I know without any doubt that whatever you may be facing, God is bigger. Regardless of how it may feel right now, He's never far away. Weeping may last for a long, dark night, but joy really does begin to grow with the first glimmering light of dawn.

Therefore we do not lose heart. Though outwardly we are wasting away, yet inwardly we are being renewed day by day. For our light and momentary troubles are achieving for us an eternal glory that far outweighs them all. So we fix our eyes not on what is seen, but on what is unseen, since what is seen is temporary, but what is unseen is eternal. (2 Corinthians 4:17-18)

When he arrived at the other side in the region of the Gadarenes, two demon-possessed men coming from the tombs met him. They were so violent that no one could pass that way. "What do you want with us, Son of God?" they shouted. "Have you come here to torture us before the appointed time?"

Some distance from them a large herd of pigs was feeding. The demons begged Jesus, "If you drive us out, send us into the herd of pigs."

He said to them, "Go!" So they came out and went into the pigs, and the whole herd rushed down the steep bank into the lake and died in the water. Those tending the pigs ran off, went into the town and reported all this, including what had happened to the demon-possessed men. Then the whole town went out to meet Jesus. And when they saw him, they pleaded with him to leave their region. (Matthew 8:28-34)

Isn't that just like us? We come so close to the miraculous but draw back. Sometimes we run away so far and so fast that we never realize how close we came to the life that Paul talks about in Philippians 3 -- the surpassing greatness of knowing Christ.

When they came face-to-face with One who could free them from the power of evil, heal their bodies, and change their hearts, the Gadarenes pled with Him to go away and leave them alone. I expect it was the prospect of change that frightened them just as change so often frightens us today. We are so afraid that we may lose our "pigs", whatever they may be.

Some of us are afraid we may have to give up doing something we enjoy. Whether it's spending weekends partying, drinking, doing drugs, etc.; or maybe it's promiscuity, idleness, or overeating. We don't want anyone telling us what we can or can't do with our bodies.

Or our pig may be a "shop 'til you drop" lifestyle. We may be obsessed with our appearance, or with expensive toys, or playing Bunco, or golf, etc. Your "pig" may be work. We don't want anyone telling us how to spend our time or money.

Our pig may be our comfort zone. If we let Christ get too close to us, He may force us to be preachers, or even worse, missionaries. He may make us give up some of our luxuries or spend time with people who are different from us. The heart of every rejection of Christ is self-centeredness. Insisting on ruling our own lives, we chase fortune and fantasies rather than opening our hearts to the amazing lives He has planned for us to live. With very narrow vision and rebellious hearts, we care more about what our "self" wants than what God wants for us.

Conversely, I know a young man who pensively welcomed Christ at a fairly young age. He is not perfect. He makes mistakes; he sins. But amid all the blunders he seeks the kingship of God, and God's righteousness. He has already had a pretty amazing life.

He has a beautiful, brilliant, humble, godly wife. Talented in her own right, she constantly lifts him up, encourages him, and honors him as part of her service to Christ. They have equally gifted children who will likely accomplish great things in the future.

He has multiple college degrees. With each change in his life's direction, like Jabez, God has regularly enlarged his territory. He has lived in many places, and will likely live in many more. He has found success in every career endeavor God has led him to pursue. He's like Joseph, always rising to the top because of the favor God gives him before men.

Their family is doing well financially right now, they have a large beautiful home with all the trimmings. But even when things were financially lean, they found contentment with the little that they had. They are faithful stewards of whatever God gives them, giving generously in their less prosperous times as well as their times of plenty.

I recently heard some of his siblings discussing how interesting his life has been. They are all highly intelligent and successful within their chosen fields. But they don't seem to have really experienced God's favor in their lives, or their careers. And none of them has found the contentment that they see in him. They seem to be somewhat "stuck" somewhere just on the verge of something, but what?

Whether your life seems dull, or you think you're doing great, you just may be standing, as Rich Mullins penned, on the verge of a miracle. You will never know what God has in store for you until you take hold of His outstretched hand and allow Him to lead you into the future that He has designed just for you. Your past is just that. It doesn't have to define your future. Remember. God is still in the business of working miracles.

But you are a chosen people, a royal priesthood, a holy nation, God's special possession, that you may declare the praises of him who called you out of darkness into his wonderful light. Once you were not a people, but now you are the people of God; once you had not received mercy, but now you have received mercy. (1 Peter 2:9-10)

God Has charged the church to stand in the gap for the world around us. Those who don't belong to Jesus Christ are deceived and lost; they are without hope and powerless to affect positive change in the world.

Meanwhile, back at the church, we seem a bit confused about our mission, and awfully selective about what we call sin. We focus too much on homosexuality, abortion, judgmentalism - too little on gossip, greed, fornication, lust, and adultery. We focus too much on organization, too little on submission; too much on planning, too little on prayer; too much on education and career plans, too little on God's Word and His plans.

Our churches are filled with people who honestly believe that they belong to Christ, but have never met the Christ they claim to serve. They have no idea that they are called to take up a cross of obedience and follow in His footsteps of self-denial, purity, integrity, and authenticity. We have been called to present a beautiful truth to a world that is perishing in a sea of lies and deception.

Too many churches, even so-called evangelical churches, have become places where people can attend their entire lives and never hear a sermon about the devastating effects of sin, their need for a Savior, or the miraculous story of God's provision.

We are failing generation after generation while wondering why our kids leave the church as soon as they enter a college or university. They have nothing to anchor them when the winds of doubt begin to blow.

The atheist professor does not appear so very different, as authority figures go, from their pastors back home. His lectures don't seem that different from the feel-good sermons they've listened to for years. They don't recognize the pull of conviction from the Holy Spirit because they don't know God. Their consciences are seared; their souls are unenlightened. Accordingly they don't recognize a lie when they meet it face to face. Tolerance is their mantra; prosperity is their goal.

At the opposite end of the spectrum are those who focus solely on sin, but only on the sins of others. They forget who the enemy is. They believe that it's homosexuals, abortionists, drunkards, pornographers, etc. Drowning

41

in legalism, they forget that those people do evil things because they are lost and headed for hell.

I appreciate those who fight the court battles against ungodly laws. That's the system of government in which God has placed us. But changing this world through the court system is not our calling.

We are called to share the whole Gospel with a hurting world. We are called to pray for and train up the next generation to know intimately the God who loves them, to believe the truth of God's Word, and to understand why they believe what they believe. We do these things so that they can then train the next generation to do the same.

If their minds are untrained or have become corrupted, their wills are weak, and their emotions are in charge, then chaos will reign and hell will be their eternal destination. The enemy has destroyed too many of our children.

The thief comes only to steal and kill and destroy; I have come that they may have life, and have it to the full. (John 10:10)

Be alert and of sober mind. Your enemy the devil prowls around looking for someone to devour. Resist him, standing firm in the faith. (1 Peter 5:8-9)

When our children were young, we had a dog that our boys named Ralph in honor of the title character in the TV series *The Greatest American Hero*. Actually, his official name was Ralph Clark Rutland; the boys were also fond of Superman.

Ralph came to us as a little tan ball of fluff that had been abandoned on a friend's doorstep in the early spring of 1981. He reminded me a little bit of the canine movie star, Benji, but on a bad hair day and with a LOT of attitude. He was loyal to a fault and very protective of our boys, who loved him very much. A terrier mix, he liked to dig and was completely undeterred by our attempts at confinement. Even a low-voltage electric wire at the base of the fence didn't stop him. You could hear him late at night yelping every time he touched the fence, but digging away nonetheless.

Ralph had a shady corner in the flower bed next to our screened porch where he had moved the mulch out of the way, and would dig down into the dirt for a cool place to nap on hot Florida days. During the summer my parents would visit along with my sister and her three young children, all of whom were a little afraid of poor Ralphie.

On one sweltering day, my dad was supervising seven of his grandchildren, our four and my sister's three, as they played in our backyard pool. Daddy watched in amusement as Ralph rose quietly from his cool corner and moved stealthily behind the hedgerow that separated the screened porch from the pool deck until he was directly opposite the diving board.

He would lie in ambush until my niece or one of her brothers would walk past his hideout en route to the diving board. Just as they passed his lair, he would dart from behind the holly bush, barking with all his might. The victim of his little prank would jump screaming into the pool, never having made it to the diving board.

Ralph would walk nonchalantly back to his corner and wait for an opportune moment to launch another "attack". According to Daddy, Ralph smiled all the way back to his lair. My dad loved to tell that story.

Ralph knew that harming any of the children was out of the question, even if they accidentally hurt him. He might growl at them, but he never bit them. He knew that the children belonged to his master. Jimmy and I had trained him from the day we got him that jumping on people or biting them was not acceptable behavior.

43

Poor Ralph had long since given up trying to scare our boys. If he barked at them for any reason they would simply chastise him; and he would stop barking and go about his business. They weren't afraid that he would hurt them because they knew that he'd been subdued by their father. They trusted their father's authority over the dog. My niece and nephews were afraid because they didn't have the same understanding of that authority.

And it always reminded me of the way Satan is with believers. He can make a lot of noise and take potshots at us, but he has been subdued by The Master.

The world seems to have come to believe that Satan is a counterpart of God; but that's not true. At best, the devil's power might be comparable to the Archangel, Michael. Both were created by God and only possess the power that God allows.

Satan can't really harm followers of Christ; but he can make them hurt themselves. He has no authority in our lives; his power is limited to what we surrender to him through our choices. Rebellion opens us up to attack because the enemy knows we are more vulnerable to his schemes the farther we stray from God.

It's a weak analogy, but a valid one. Had my niece and nephews bothered to stand their ground rather than running away, the game would have been over. Ralph would not have found scaring them worth his time and energy had he not gotten the desired response.

God's power is not limited by time, distance, or even our conduct. He can rescue us from any malady, even those of our own making. But He will often allow us to learn the hard way the folly of straying, if we choose not to learn it any other way.

Years ago I knew a young couple who were both believers; but they had strayed far from God. The symptoms of their rebellion were displayed in sexual immorality, partying, and even dabbling in drugs. They were experiencing strange phenomena at their house, lights turning on with no one flipping a switch, etc. Events that would scare them, but never really harm them. One of them told me that when I would come into their house, things would become peaceful. It was not my presence so much as the presence of the Holy Spirit that made the difference. I am no threat to anyone. But the minions of Hell cower in the presence of the Spirit of the living God.

The next time we are tempted to stray into fearfulness, or some other stronghold of sin, it would be wise to stop and remember who the true

Master is. He died on a cross 2000 years ago so that neither sin nor Satan would have power over us.

Therefore God exalted Him to the highest place and gave Him the name that is above every name, that at the name of Jesus every knee should bow, in heaven and on earth and under the earth, and every tongue acknowledge that Jesus Christ is Lord, to the glory of God the Father. (Philippians 2:9-11)

So, whenever we are confronted with the enemy's schemes, whether it's temptation, real danger, or just a lot of scary-sounding noise, if we will call on the name of Jesus, He will show up, and the enemy will flee from His presence - and he won't be smiling.

When Jesus underwent testing in the wilderness, He set the standard for us by using God's written word to rebuke the devil. We cannot lose a spiritual battle if we are filled with the Holy Spirit and armed with the Word of God. After all it's not our battle to fight. In Christ, that war has already been won. If you belong to Christ, it's a good time to be a name-dropper.

Submit yourselves then to God. Resist the devil and he will flee from you. Come near to God and He will come near to you. ...Humble yourselves before the Lord and He will lift you up. (James 1:7-8, 10)

Sometime later, Jesus went up to Jerusalem for one of the Jewish festivals. Now there is in Jerusalem near the Sheep Gate a pool, which in Aramaic is called Bethesda and which is surrounded by five covered colonnades. Here a great number of disabled people used to lie - the blind, the lame, the paralyzed. One who was there had been an invalid for thirty-eight years. When Jesus saw him lying there and learned he had been in this condition a long time, He said to him, "Do you want to get well?" (John 5:1-6)

Sadly, many people don't seem to want to get well (or be made whole) either physically or spiritually. Physical healing might bring a loss of attention or sympathy. Spiritual wholeness might bring a loss of relationships, require us to change some area of our lives, or give up a pet sin or habit. Healing would require authenticity before God. We have to be willing to be honest about our need and the desires of our hearts. Wholeness would surely require submission to Christ.

Jesus didn't impose healing on the lame man, or even assume that it was wanted; He simply asked. His question addressed a deeper need in the lame man, a need to examine his heart. In much the same way, He searches the hearts of those He encounters today. He already knows how we'll respond, but He asks anyway. He wants us to examine our own hearts. Do we really want Him to make us whole? Is some hidden sin or fear holding us back? He offers, but we must decide.

"Sir," the invalid replied, "I have no one to help me into the pool when the water is stirred. While I am trying to get in someone else goes down ahead of me."

Then Jesus said to him, "Get up! Pick up your mat and walk." At once the man was cured; he picked up his mat and walked. (John 5:7-9)

Like the invalid I have made many excuses to God for the insecurities that have plagued me for most of my life. The truth is that it does not matter how mistreated we may have been, how many times we have been hurt, who has betrayed us, or how unhappy we have become. What matters is where we go with the hard circumstances of our lives. Do we sit on the sidelines and wait for some person to come and rescue us from the misery that we've permitted to define our lives? Or do we take hold of that nail-scarred hand that is extended to us in love, the hand that made the lame to walk and the blind to see?

Can there be any greater cruelty than placing the burden for our happiness on another human being. Only in a relationship with Christ can we find contentment, completeness, and joy – the building blocks of love? What more proof of His love could there be than He has already provided?

46

When we finally get over ourselves we can begin to give ourselves wholly to Him. He only heals what we give Him. If you doubt who He is or what He has done simply pick up your Bible, open it to the Gospel of John, ask God to reveal Himself to you, and start reading. You will find all the Truth, all the love, and all the healing that your heart desires.

Every encounter with Christ begins with an examination of the depths of our hearts. He looks into the darkest places where we try to hide the broken, hardened, or scarred remnants of past failures, sins, or hurts. It is into those places that He shines His healing light. It is in those places where healing begins. He graciously offers forgiveness, freedom, and healing; but just as with salvation, we have to want healing and we have to accept it.

The day on which this took place was a Sabbath, and so the Jewish leaders said to the man who had been healed, "It is the Sabbath; the law forbids you to carry your mat."

But he replied, "The man who made me well said to me, 'Pick up your mat and walk.'"

So they asked him, "Who is this fellow who told you to pick it up and walk?" The man who was healed had no idea who it was, for Jesus had slipped away into the crowd that was there. (John 5:9-12)

Often the visible change in our lives and demeanor will be noticeable to the people around us providing us opportunities to share the reason for the changes. This introduces others to the One who can change their lives as well, and it reinforces for us the truth of what He has done - so that we don't lose sight of the miracle.

Later Jesus found him at the temple and said to him, "See, you are well again. Stop sinning or something worse may happen to you." The man went away and told the Jewish leaders that it was Jesus who had made him well. (John 5:14-15)

I have no idea what sin Jesus challenged the man to stop. Jesus is like that; He dealt with that issue later, one-on-one, away from the crowd. His purpose for us is repentance and victory over sin, not public shame or humiliation. I don't think Jesus was giving him an "or else" ultimatum, but rather a warning of the dangers that awaited one whose physical activity has been limited, but now would find the whole world open to him. Jesus sought him out to demonstrate love that created a miracle so that, understanding the value that God placed on him, he would not return to a life of defeat, self-pity, and self-loathing. How about you; do you want to get well?

And we know that in all things God works for the good of those who love Him, who have been called according to His purpose. (Romans 8:28)

I heard the story of a young man who was going a through a very difficult time of loss and heartache. He ended up having to serve a couple of months in jail. While he was there, the food he had purchased from the canteen to supplement his meals was stolen. Since they were allowed only one visit per week to the canteen, the man was disheartened at the prospect of a long, hungry week. But he decided to go about business as usual. He didn't report the theft nor did he treat the thief differently than he treated anyone else.

The jail facility was arranged dormitory-style, and meals were served through an opening in the door. The residents lined up in no particular order to receive their trays. There was no way for an employee or inmate to know who would get which tray, and no one else in the dorm received extra food. But the man whose food had been stolen received extra food on his tray each day.

The others in the dorm noticed the difference in his food portions just as they had noticed the difference in his reaction to the theft. They began to question him about the devotional materials he read each day, which he was able to share with some of them. When he was released he gave the Bible that his mom had sent him to another inmate. One who was going to be there for a long time.

Returning to his former life with the same old temptations, he found himself at a crossroad. Would he forget the miraculous nature of the personal, yet public, provision for his needs? Would he remember how God had drawn near in his time of distress, or return to full-on rebellion against God? Would he once again allow himself to be pushed and pulled by temptations and circumstances? Or would he decide to get well and cling to the One who brings genuine health and wholeness? The choice was his alone.

Just as with any relationship, the quality of our relationship with God is determined by the time we spend with Him. In studying the Word we get to know God and learn of His faithfulness and power. Through prayer, we are made aware as those attributes are made manifest in our daily lives.

As the old song says, we spend our lives, looking for love in all the wrong places. We often rely on imperfect human relationships which bring temporal happiness, rather than drawing near to the One who can bring true peace, contentment, and joy both now and forever. People are flawed, sooner or later they will fail you. Christ never will.

To the one who draws near in repentance He promises: *I will give you a new heart and put a new spirit in you; I will remove from you your heart of stone and give you a heart of flesh and I will put my Spirit in you and move you to follow my decrees and be careful to keep my laws. Then you will live in the land I gave your ancestors; you will be my people, and I will be your God. I will save you from all your uncleanness. (Ezekiel 36:26-29)*

The Bible is meant to be bread for our daily use, not just cake for special occasions. – Unknown

There is a way that seems right to a man and appears straight before him, but at the end of it is the way of death. (Proverbs 14:12)

We live in a rural area where traffic still comes to a halt for a funeral procession, and the county fair still opens with a parade. I remember one really fun evening at the fair with two of our grandchildren, Grant and Ella, along with their parents and the rest of their adoring entourage. At ages 4 and 2 the children were wide-eyed with delight at the sights, sounds, food, and rides that are "the fair".

They looked at every farm animal and rode every kiddie ride at the fair, some repeatedly. One especially sweet moment was the first time the two of them rode the "teacup" ride. Their mom, Amanda, told Grant that if Ella got scared he should sit close to her so that she could touch him. As the ride started to move she was clearly apprehensive. Grant was watching her, and as fear welled up in her eyes, he slid closer to her and put his little hand on her arm.

As the ride progressed she was still a bit tense and he slid over as close as he could get to her, eventually ending up with his arm around her shoulders like a little man. Around they went, two tiny tow-headed angels. As he talked quietly to her she relaxed and began to smile and actually enjoy the ride.

In the same way, amidst of the chaos that marks 21st-Century America, there is an extended hand and the gentle whisper, "Come to me". Jesus offers love, peace, joy, hope, and grace to all who will respond to His invitation.

Grace is free to us, but it cost Jesus dearly. He paid with a lifetime of obedience to God and faithfulness to His mission. He paid with suffering and humiliation; allowing himself to be tortured, stripped naked, and publicly murdered. His was an exemplary life of obedience to God. He was the perfect example for our lives and sacrifice for our sin.

Rejecting God's leadership in daily life is evidence of our rebellion against His rightful position as LORD of all. In our rights-oriented society people often bristle at the idea of Lordship. But surrender is the natural result of getting to know Christ in proper relationship.

Jesus is LORD whether I choose to surrender to Him, or to rebel against Him. He carried the sin of the world upon His shoulders as He climbed a hill called Golgotha. If you surrender yourself completely into His care, He will lift you up, burdens and all, and never leave you forlorn.

In times of trouble He draws near to bring comfort, hope, and healing. He removes the guilt of your past; and He gives wisdom and strength to deal with the leftover baggage.

His Word encourages us: *Do not be anxious about anything, but with prayer and supplication with thanksgiving make your requests known to God. And the peace of God which surpasses all understanding will guard your hearts and your minds in Christ Jesus. (Philippians 4:6-7)*

In this chaotic world, I gladly bow to a Savior who notices when I am hurt or afraid and will come close, gently put His arm around me and whisper words of love, comfort, forgiveness, and healing.

Come to me all you who are weary and burdened, and I will give you rest. Take my yoke upon you and learn from me, for I am gentle and humble in heart, and you will find rest for your souls. For my yoke is easy and my burden is light." (Matthew 11:28-30)

In addition to all this, take up the shield of faith, with which you will be able to extinguish all the flaming arrows of the evil one. (Ephesians 6:16)

The word "shield" in this verse comes from the Greek work thyreos, which refers to a large, curved, door-like shield such as the scutum used by the Roman soldiers who occupied much of the known world during Paul's lifetime. It was usually constructed of wood, sometimes covered with leather and often had bronze bands at the edges to keep it from splitting. It was quite effective on the battlefield when an army was under assault from distant enemy archers.

Under a particularly heavy barrage, the soldiers were able to overlap the edges and kneel behind the "wall" while others of their legion would hold their shields over their heads creating a testudo (Latin for tortoise) which offered protection from high-flying missiles and arrows.

Our faith functions in much the same way when Satan hurls fiery accusations, lies, words of discouragement - all aimed at destroying our effectiveness as believers. It's very hard to live out God's mandate to share His love with those around us when Satan is constantly reminding us of our past failures, whispering that the one who needs to hear will reject us, or lying about God's ability or willingness to work in any given situation.

The Shield of Faith is constructed of Grace, plain and simple. Grace says that it does not matter what I have done in the past or what my inadequacies may be, God loves me and He is able to use me to accomplish His purpose.

Grace says that the Cross of Christ secures once and for eternity my status as one who is covered with the righteousness of Christ. When I call on His name, He will always come to my rescue - not because I deserve rescue, but because Christ's sacrifice for me demands it. Grace says that He never leaves me alone in times of darkness. And when the greatest assaults come, He provides the words for our defense and often brings other people of faith alongside to combine their faith with mine and help me to stand firm in the battle.

If you are under assault from the enemy right now, know that God loves you. Know that Jesus died for you. Know that if you call on Him, He will come to your defense. And know that this was written because God wants you to know that there are others standing with you and praying for you. I just did.

It shall come to pass that before they call, I will answer; and while they are still speaking, I will hear. (Isaiah 65:24)

When Jesus saw His mother there, and the disciple whom he loved standing nearby, He said to her, "Woman, here is your son", and to the disciple, "Here is your mother". (John 19:26-27)

The scripture tells us nothing about Mary at the cross, except that she was present, that John was nearby, and that Jesus was concerned for her welfare. We can probably assume that she knew Jesus better than any other person on earth. She knew that He was born to a virgin. Many of us think our children are perfect, she knew her eldest son was. She knew He could work miracles; she sent for Him when there was only water left to drink at a wedding in Cana. I believe she had experienced too many miracles to think that anything was beyond God's control. She knew who His Father was.

I'm sure she grieved for her son, and was very likely in shock and horrified at what she was seeing. But I also believe that our loving God, who had handpicked her to be His mother, surely extended His miraculous grace to enable her to see it through to the end.

I know that the two can't really be compared. But any mother who has watched her child depart to serve God in a place where they arrest, torture, and sometimes kill people just for sharing the gospel of Christ, knows that God gives you a deep understanding of His plan for that child. She has received the grace to accept God's ownership of her child's future.

Mary was both His mother, and His child. God's ministry in her life must have been greater than we can begin to comprehend. She had been surrendered to God's will for more than 33 years. I doubt that she balked at the completion of it. In such an extreme turn of events, all that I know of God's character tells me that He probably provided extreme grace.

Mary was present, but Jesus didn't die cradled in her loving arms. He died completely alone, pushing against a spike that had been driven into His feet, just to get a breath of air. Each push would have caused his torn and bloody back to rub against the rough-hewn wood of the cross. Each time He exhaled, His hands must have pulled against the nails that were driven through them as His body slumped in exhaustion. Each movement of His head drove the thorns deeper into His skull.

And if all this were not enough, He held the burden of my sin in those outstretched arms. The ugliness of my sin caused God to turn His face away, which meant that He did it all without the comfort or strength He had always found in His Father's presence. He took my sin and covered me with His righteousness so that I would never have to endure being forsaken by God.

The crucifixion of Jesus of Nazareth, the Christ, was referenced by a number of secular historical figures including a Roman historian named Tacitus, a Hebrew historian named Josephus, and is mentioned in the Babylonian Talmud.

Christ's death was the supreme act of obedience. He didn't have to submit to any of it. The soldiers didn't arrest Him in the garden, He surrendered to them. He set the example of what it means to be a child of God: to live a life of submission to God's plan so that His will may be done, and He will be glorified on earth. To be crucified with Christ is to lay my sin and my selfish desires at His nail-scarred feet and allow Him to cover me with His cleansing blood.

I have been crucified with Christ and I no longer live, but Christ lives in me. The life I live in the body, I live by faith in the son of God, who loved me and gave Himself for me. I do not set aside the grace of God, for if righteousness could be gained through the law, Christ died for nothing. (Galatians 3:20-21)

At the beginning the Creator made them male and female, and said, "For this reason a man will leave his father and mother and be united to his wife, and the two will become one flesh. So they are no longer two, but one. Therefore what God has joined together, let man not separate." (Matthew 19:4-6)

"Dearly beloved, we are gathered together here in the sight of God, and in the face of this company, to join together this Man and this Woman in holy Matrimony; which is an honorable estate, instituted of God, signifying unto us the mystical union that is between Christ and his Church ...and therefore is not by any to be entered into unadvisedly or lightly; but reverently, discreetly, advisedly, soberly, and in the fear of God."

Almost every marriage ceremony I've ever attended began with those words from The Book of Common Prayer. Yet so many couples do enter into it foolishly, lightly, and without the fear of God. Even many in the Church have adopted an attitude that says, "If it doesn't work out we can always get a divorce." Or the attitude displayed by one young woman I know who completely missed the sacred oneness of marriage. She stood before God and took vows that she had no intention of keeping. In her upside down belief system her relationships with God and her husband both followed her children and her mother on her list of priorities.

Society, even many people who call themselves Christians, have discarded the teachings of Christ in favor of what they deem socially acceptable. Divorce has become more common that marital faithfulness. We call them "single-parent homes" rather than the broken families that they are. One of the tragedies of the "women's movement" is that it has so often become the wife who abandons her marriage.

What can we expect when even so-called Christian leaders behave no differently? I was dumbfounded to hear a famous Christian performer publicly proclaim that she had "tried everything" to save her marriage. Her husband was also a Christian who wanted to keep his family together. Apparently she tried everything except choosing to keep her vows. Of course she would have had to end her "friendship" with the man she later married. Instead, she slandered God by effectively telling the world that God cannot save a marriage, even when two Christians want Him to. I wonder how many Christian couples have stumbled over her words on their way to divorce court.

When those whom God has joined together and sealed in a covenant relationship decide to separate, the result is rather like what would happen if conjoined twins decided to cut themselves apart. You would find two badly wounded people, at least one of whom would likely be destroyed.

Beyond the spiritual oneness of the marriage relationship, there is a physical oneness that is equally impossible to dissolve. Scientists now understand that DNA from a woman's sexual partners is absorbed by her at a cellular level, remaining in her blood, brain, and heart tissue for years (perhaps all her life) in a process known as microchimerism. They've known for a while that male DNA shows up in the tissue of women who have given birth to sons, fetal microchimerism. Adds a whole new dimension to what mothers knew already, our children literally live on in our hearts. I won't go into all the things it explains about what has happened to my brain with the birth of each subsequent son, but it explains a lot!

But recent studies have confirmed the same phenomenon in some women who have never had a son, some who have never had a child at all. They list some possible explanations as an unknown brother who never developed in the womb, an unknown early miscarriage, or her sexual partners. So, in a very real sense, the fact that you are actually having sex with everyone your partner has ever had sex with belies the notion of casual sex. It seems logical that DNA could be transferred at least as easily through such intimate contact as is disease. It sometimes strikes me as almost humorous how science continues to confirm scripture. So many of man's greatest "discoveries" are just footnotes of biblical truth.

Jesus gave only one situation in which God dissolves a marriage relationship: unrepentant adultery. I emphasize unrepentant because He also made it clear that we are required to forgive those who sin against us, and be restored to anyone who repents of their sins against us. I think that applies to the marriage relationship at least as much as it applies to any other relationship. In those very rare situations where God permits divorce He acts as a master surgeon delicately separating the one back into two who can become whole and complete. But there will always be scars.

Because only God can make two into one, only He can separate them. Only He can break His seal. Marriage perfectly exemplifies Christ's relationship with His Bride in that, at the moment of our Salvation we become one with Christ. No one can separate us from Him. In order for you to turn your back on your marriage, you must first turn your back on God. Despite society's confusion on the issue, there really is no gray area here.

I believe that when God looks at a married couple, He sees the complete "One" that He created when He joined them together. It is a mystery and

56

hard for us to understand, but not for the Triune God – the Father, Son, and Holy Spirit – three separate beings, but One Holy God.

Perhaps if we were capable of understanding the Mystery of the Trinity, it would be easier to understand just how personal the marriage relationship is to God. In Malachi's day, the people of Israel were mourning over God's refusal to accept their offerings.

Malachi's explanation: *It is because the Lord is acting as the witness between you and the wife (or husband) of your youth, because you have broken faith with her, though she is your partner, the wife of your marriage covenant.*

Has not the Lord made them one? In flesh and spirit they are His. . . . So guard yourself in your spirit, and do not break faith with the wife (or husband) of your youth. I hate divorce, says the Lord God of Israel, and I hate a man's covering himself with violence. . . . So guard yourself in your spirit, and do not break faith. (Malachi 2:14-16)

For you created my inmost being; you knit me together in my mother's womb. I praise you because I am fearfully and wonderfully made; your works are wonderful, I know that full well. My frame was not hidden from you when I was made in the secret place, when I was woven together in the depths of the earth. Your eyes saw my unformed body; all the days ordained for me were written in your book before one of them came to be. How amazing are your thoughts concerning me, God! How vast is the sum of them! (Psalm 139:13-17)

We had dinner a while back at a little Japanese restaurant to celebrate the birthday of my great-niece, Mackenzie. She's a lovely young lady with her daddy's eyes, smile, and gentle soul. It tugs at the hurt of losing him, but still warms my heart to see him in his "little princess' face". He was such a great father who loved God and his family more than anything.

But that evening was filled with much joy as many of our family gathered to rejoice together in Mackenzie's life. I was surrounded by "greats", two great nephews and five great nieces. Of course the center of attention is always the current baby; that night it was little Ella Grace who was born with Trisomy 21, or Down Syndrome.

An oversimplification of Trisomy 21 is that an extra copy of Chromosome 21 from either the mother's egg or the father's sperm occurs, usually before fertilization takes place. Down Syndrome brings with it a wide range of possible health challenges.

Dr. Brian Skotko, a board-certified medical geneticist, is Co-director of the Down Syndrome Program at Massachusetts General Hospital. He estimates that more than 90% of Down Syndrome babies are aborted each year, a tragic loss to the world, especially to the parents who have no idea what they've missed. I've known a number of people who were created with that extra chromosome, and they are among the most loving, guileless, funny, and gracious people I know.

Following is an excerpt from a letter I wrote to Ella Grace's parents a few days after her birth:

Congratulations on the birth of your beautiful little daughter, Ella Grace! I know you must be exhausted by the strain of dealing with the unknown and the weight of making tough decisions. You've been thrust into the hardest parts of parenthood in such a short time. After watching Linda these last four years I'm absolutely certain of three things: that God is bigger than anything that we face, He never wastes pain, and when things seem hardest is when He draws nearest.

He knit little Ella Grace together in your womb with as much care and just as perfectly as every other child He creates. She is wonderfully made and perfectly designed to

58

fulfill God's purpose for her. Doctors make diagnoses and people want to put labels on those who are different from the norm. But different does not mean defective. Each child is unique. Ella Grace is exactly who God designed her to be, and He rejoices with you in her beauty. The words He speaks over her are certainly, "Sweet Ella Grace, I know the plans I have for you. They are plans to bless you and never to harm you, plans to give you hope and a future".

None of us may understand this side of Heaven why she has suffered so much in these first few weeks of her life, but God does. You may never know how many lives are touched by her story. These are days to treasure in your hearts just as surely as all the joyful days that await your little family in the future. I believe there will be many Happy Birthdays, Merry Christmases, Mother's Days, Father's Days, and days to celebrate the births of her little siblings. These hard days, just as all the ones to come, will all work together for good for your little family. And while she is enduring much pain right now, she won't remember the pain, only the loving care she is receiving from her parents will stay with her into the future.

Although we may never in our natural lives know what it is, I believe with all my heart that God has a plan for every child who was ever conceived. There are no accidents; He does not make mistakes. The fact that our worldly perspective makes it difficult for us to comprehend just what He is doing does not mean that He is not at work. Each child is a person, created in God's image. Things that we view as flaws are, in fact, God's signature on His precious masterpiece. We are creations upon whom God can gaze and see His image — a reflection of Himself.

My dear children, I write this to you so that you will not sin. But if anybody does sin, we have an advocate with the Father - Jesus Christ, the Righteous One. He is the atoning sacrifice for our sins, and not only for ours but also for the sins of the whole world.

We know that we have come to know Him if we keep His commands. Whoever says, "I know Him", but does not do what He commands is a liar, and the truth is not in that person. But if anyone obeys His word, love for God is truly made complete in them. This is how we know we are in Him; whoever claims to live in Him must live as Jesus did. (1 John 2:2-6)

This passage contains some very hard truth. If the Body of Christ would live as Jesus did, we would be living in a very different world than we see around us today. He gave us His Word and His Spirit so that we can know Him. If we, who are called by His name don't allow God's word to change us, why would we think it could change those around us?

We can know that God's Word is trustworthy just as He is trustworthy. Almost every archaeological discovery in the Middle East produces new confirmation of the historical accuracy of the scriptures. There is a thread of prophecy that runs through the scriptures, stitching ancient history together, whereby the Bible actually authenticates itself. Individually and collectively, the books of the Bible point to Jesus Christ. Genesis to Revelation, the Bible is His story. History is His story.

But even within the church God's Word is no longer given the honor it deserves. By pulling verses out of context and ignoring the passages with which they don't agree, false prophets and lukewarm church members deny the authority of the Scriptures. Thus, they are leading a lost and hurting world down a slippery slope of deception that is devoid of practical solutions to life's most difficult dilemmas.

By relying on human understanding, the deceived elevate the false prophet to the status of god. Meanwhile the lukewarm lead lives of vanity, treading merrily down the garden path toward certain destruction, oblivious to the emptiness of their relationships with God. Honestly, I've never talked to a productive Christian who said he was content with his relationship with God. They always express a desire for more.

It is in this hunger for more of Him, more of His character, more of His righteousness where growth begins. It is in the process of knowing Him that His will is discerned. He leads step by step and day by day.

God is merciful and loving. But He is equally just, righteous, Holy, and wrathful. Because He is righteous, He cannot tolerate sin. Because He is just,

His wrath requires a blood sacrifice. Because He is merciful, His wrath was poured out on His Son.

The death and resurrection of Christ is the single biggest event that has happened since God created the heavens and the earth, but is often treated so casually that people forget that it brings a life or death decision to everybody on the face of the earth.

His sacrifice is so great that He extends His gift of salvation only to those who take it seriously. He requires His children to commit to Him and allow His love to change them. *How much more severely do you think someone deserves to be punished who has trampled the Son of God underfoot, who has treated as an unholy thing the blood of the covenant that sanctified them, and who has insulted the Spirit of grace? (Hebrews 10:29)*

How then should we live? The answer is simple, but not always easy: *Trust in the Lord with all your heart and lean not on your own understanding; in all your ways submit to Him and He will guide you on the right paths. (Proverbs 3:5-6)*

Do not be misled: Bad company corrupts good character. Come back to your senses as you ought, and stop sinning. (1 Corinthians 15:33-34)

I wish he would come to his senses, or something like it, is a phrase we often hear these days. It's usually said of someone whose lifestyle has deviated from his personal norm. To me it expresses a desire to see them experience freedom from the destruction that lies in the spiritual realm of rebellion against God.

It became my prayer when people close to me abandoned spouses and devastated their children in pursuit of adulterous relationships; and it was repeated when other loved ones began partying, began using drugs, or began sacrificing family relationships to careers.

Luke 15:11-32 tells the story of the prodigal son who rebelled against his father, took his inheritance, and pursued a hedonistic lifestyle that belied the values of his family heritage. As his money dwindled so did the number of so-called friends who had partied with him on his way down.

At last he found himself destitute in a foreign land, working in a pigsty, where he finally came to his senses. As he made his way back to his father's house, he rehearsed the plea he would make for forgiveness and the request he would make for a servant's job. Instead, he found grace, mercy and full restoration. In his father's eyes the prodigal had never been disowned nor forgotten.

I wonder if the prodigal would ever have come to his senses if his father had not allowed him to suffer the full consequences of his choices. I've seen parents physically assist their child multiple times in moving out of the marriage home, which was promptly abandoned as soon as they met the next "significant other". Others have provided a love nest for a child in an immoral relationship. Still another family helped to financially support their daughter and grandson even though she was exposing her child to a completely immoral lifestyle of lying, stealing, partying, and drugs - even exchanging sex for drugs.

All of these are Christian parents who were afraid of losing their child's affection had they dared to simply say, "Honor your vows. Work things out with your spouse. What you are doing is wrong and I will not offend God by helping you down this path of rebellion." Instead they bear the guilt of their complicity in the destruction of homes, and harm done to their own grandchildren. It is much better to offend your wayward child than to offend Almighty God.

In 1 Corinthians 15:33-34, Paul was addressing the Christians, believers who had strayed into sinful lifestyles, destroying fellowship with God and the possibility of sharing Truth with those around them.

Again in 2 Timothy 2, Paul admonishes followers of Christ to *Flee the evil desires of youth, and pursue righteousness, faith, love and peace, along with those who call on the Lord out of a pure heart... and that they will come to their senses and escape from the trap of the devil, who has taken them captive to do his will.*

Over the course of the last two decades, we've seen a number of prominent men of God fall away from intimacy with God and into sin. Repeated hardening of the heart toward God's Word and the work of His Spirit leads to a dulling of the senses. It affects not only our ability to hear God's voice, but also compassion and sensitivity to the needs of others, producing a heart of stone.

As I've learned in my own journey through spiritual palaces and pigpens, the weight of carrying a hardened heart is physically and spiritually exhausting. But, when repentance comes, I have always found the Father waiting for me with healing and restoration, never condemnation.

Repentance is painful, but not nearly so painful as the emptiness of separation from Christ. And the joy that I find in His presence is so very worth the pain of repentance. Just as God promised the Israelites in Ezekiel's day, He still promises the penitent prodigal:

For I will cleanse you from all your impurities and from all your idols. I will give you a new heart and put a new spirit in you; I will remove from you your heart of stone and give you a heart of flesh. And I will put my Spirit in you and move you to follow my decrees and be careful to keep my laws. You will live in the land I gave your forefathers; you will be my people, and I will be your God. I will save you from all your uncleanness. (Ezekiel 36:26-29)

*Many men owe the grandeur
of their lives to their tremendous
difficulties.*

-C. H. Spurgeon

Part Three

Not a burden we bear,
Not a sorrow we share,
But our toil He doth richly repay;
Not a grief or a loss,
Not a frown or a cross,
But is blest if we trust and obey.

God is our refuge and strength, a very present help in trouble. (Psalm 46:1)

It's rarely good news when the phone rings early in the morning, and this call would be no exception. For the second time in just over a year we were both unemployed and wondering just what the Lord had in store for us next. We could never have guessed what had already happened and how the world as we knew it had shattered overnight.

For the past year I had the joy of spending 3 days each week with our fourth grandson, Grant. Pop had gotten up early and headed over to bring Grant back to our house for what promised to be a fun-filled day. I was up, dressed and headed for the den, Bible in hand, to prepare for our day together.

It was 6:34 AM on August 25, 2008 when the phone began to ring. As I picked up the handset I saw my sister's number on the caller ID and hoped everything was alright. Georgia's voice was strained; I could hear the shock and confusion in her voice as she said, "A friend, who works at EMS, just called. He said there's been a shooting at Linda's house. He said a male is dead and a female has been transported to the hospital." I had always thought movie scenes where women swoon or become weak in the knees at traumatic moments were melodramatic. I was wrong.

I don't remember anything else about the phone call. As I sank to my knees I picked up the remote on the night stand next to the phone and switched on the television. It was true. There was a reporter standing in the road in front of the yellow crime scene tape that surrounded the house that Linda and Philip had built some 40 years earlier. I listened in disbelief as she reported that there were two deceased males and that a female had also been shot and transported to the hospital.

I called Georgia back and told her about the television news report. She said, "It's Carey." I breathed a brief, but as I was soon to learn, very powerful prayer, "God, I can't do this. Please, Help me." He did. I think that He created shock, that physical state when emotional trauma destroys your ability to think straight, so that we would be unable to fight Him while He tenderly carries us through the worst moments of our lives.

While I was trying desperately to convince myself that this was real and not some horrific nightmare, I managed to go about the business of preparing. I was able to catch Jimmy before Nathaniel and Amanda, Grant's mom and dad, left for work. I told him what had happened and that he needed to come home so that we could go to the hospital. I even managed to pack a few essentials that I would need as I stayed at the hospital, although

I don't remember doing it. I had no idea what Linda's condition was, but the Lord knew I was staying the night at the hospital.

It was a dismal, rainy morning as though the heavens felt our anguish. You could almost touch the darkness that descended on us as reality sank in. Every moment felt like an eternity. The rush-hour drive to Memorial University Medical Center some 35 miles away in Savannah seemed to take forever. We even had to wait for a train. The kind of evil I'd only heard about had entered my world, and I knew life would never be the same.

As I write this, that horrible night was more than five years ago, and I can say with absolute certainty that, regardless of what you may be facing today, God is bigger. Linda's prayer as she lay bleeding on her bedroom floor was that same heart's cry, God, I can't do this. If I'm going to make it, You will have to carry me.

I've watched Him carry Linda through so many surgeries I've lost count; constant pain; physical and occupational therapy; losing her husband, her youngest son, and her home; the trial and conviction of her oldest son; having to watch the perpetrators proudly flaunting the betrayal; and I saw her fight to protect her grandchildren, taking them into her home, and caring for them even when she wasn't physically able to do so.

And always she has depended on God for the strength, grace, and peace to get through one more minute of one more day. Only God could do that. What He did for her, He will gladly do for you, just pray that same little prayer, God, I can't do this. Please, help me. He is there. He loves you. He will answer.

Don't boast about tomorrow, for you don't know what a day might bring. (Proverbs 27:1)

It can be frightening just how fragile life can be. It's been just over five years now since my world was turned upside down. When a shadowy figure entered my sister's home in the middle of the night, he left behind far more than just shattered lives. He left the stark realization that nothing, not even life itself, could ever again be taken for granted.

Death comes to all of us. Philip and Carey would have died eventually. We all will. When it comes to the aged or those who suffer long, painful diseases, death can bring both comfort and heartbreak to those left behind. When death comes because of some natural disaster or accident, the shock and trauma can be almost unbearable. But death holds a special horror when it is deliberate, treacherous, and violent – striking in the quiet hours of rest.

I remember vividly the first time I went back to my sister's house after that night. So little looked different (at least at first); and yet everything had changed. My heart still grows heavy when I think about the guest bathroom where, laid out neatly on the vanity, were the items my nephew had prepared for the next day. It was probably the last thing he did before he went to bed that night. Despite his broken heart and shattered dreams, he still believed that he would have a tomorrow.

You don't even know what tomorrow will bring -- what your life will be! For you are like smoke that appears for a little while, then vanishes. (James 4:14)

I can't begin to understand why God allows such events in the lives of His children. Carey was an authentic follower of Christ, and growing deeper in Him, even as his life was falling apart. His last thoughts as he drifted off that night were likely a prayer for his children. He was that kind of man, that kind of dad. It was such a tragic loss to all his family and friends.

I think his dad, Philip, sensed that he would be gone soon. He said his goodbyes to some extended family members in the days just before the end. A heart attack wouldn't have surprised him, but I doubt he dreamed his life would end violently.

But I know that God is good. I have experienced firsthand His faithfulness, even in the very darkest moments of my life. I've learned that the worst of storms are only temporary. However dark the clouds, loud the thunder, intense the lightning, rough the waves, or mighty the winds, they still recognize God's voice. In this case, He didn't physically raise the dead (yet). But still I know that they live and I will see them again.

Therefore I tell you do not worry about your life, what you will eat or drink; or your body, what you will wear. But seek first His kingdom and His righteousness, and all these things will be given to you as well. (Matthew 6:25, 33)

We waste so much time fretting about insignificant things. Even our most fundamental needs seem trivial when we are faced with the frailty of today. It's often the most traumatic moments of our lives that cause us to pause and take stock of where we are, and why we are. We were made for far greater things than most of us will ever begin to imagine. Our reason for living involves far more than earning a living, deciding where to live, what to wear, what to eat, or whom we will marry.

We were created to glorify God with our lives. God's plans for us involve things that will cause the people we encounter along the way to sit up and notice Him. His dreams for us are far bigger than anything we could begin to dream, or even imagine. He gifted each of us uniquely to be equipped for the work He has for us - to live the life that He gives us today.

I am sure most of us would be terrified if the Lord revealed His plans in advance. And so He reveals it step by step and day by day. And with His daily direction, He provides the wisdom, the strength, and the courage we need to pull it off. In the process, He remakes each of us from the inside out, revealing the people He has always known we could be.

God knows us too well to expect this development of His character in us to be a quick or easy process. He only expects us to walk in the understanding that we already have. As we surrender to the light we have been given, He gives more light, more understanding, and a slightly bigger pond in which to fish.

I've noticed that the people I see walk closest to God lead the most fulfilling, and often, the most interesting lives. Whether you call it progressive sanctification or simply maturing in our faith, the purpose and the result are the same – to become the people God made us to be. People who reflect His image, bring glory to His name, and are fit to spend eternity with Him in His heaven.

Not that I have already reached the goal or am already fully mature, but I make every effort to take hold of it because I also have been taken hold of by Christ Jesus. Brothers, I do not consider myself to have taken hold of it. But one thing I do: Forgetting what is behind and reaching forward to what is ahead, I pursue as my goal the prize promised by God's heavenly call in Christ Jesus....In any case, we should live up to whatever truth we have attained. (Philippians 3:12-14, 16)

69

As we follow Christ, much as He provided manna to the Hebrew people as they journeyed from slavery in Egypt to their promised land, He provides what we need today on our journey from being lost in our sin to our own promised eternity with Him.

...and your strength will equal your days. (Deuteronomy 33:25)

Though He slay me, yet will I hope in Him. (Job 13:15)

ebuchadnezzar had laid siege to Jerusalem and conquered Israel. He'd plundered the Temple of God, carrying away its treasures to Babylon. He sent one of his court officials to bring young men from the royal family and nobility, the most fit and educated, so that they could serve him.

Among the captives were Hananiah, Mishael, and Azariah. Given Babylonian names - Shadrach, Meshach, and Abednego, they were to be fed the richest of foods and wine from the king's own table. They would spend three years being trained before entering his service. These three, all friends of Daniel from Judah, distinguished themselves in wisdom and understanding of the Babylonian culture and literature they were given to study.

Isolated from family and others who shared their faith, bowing to government and peer pressure to conform to the culture into which they had been reluctantly thrust would have been the easy choice. Instead they chose to remain faithful to the One whom they knew to be the only true God. They refused to adapt to the pagan culture including the king's rich food and wine, which had been offered in worship to idols. They chose instead to eat a diet of fresh vegetables and water. God blessed their faithfulness and they were elevated to positions of leadership in the government of Babylon.

Nebuchadnezzar had commissioned an idol to be made of gold, ninety feet high and nine feet wide and summoned all the government officials to attend the dedication. He decreed that anyone who refused to worship the idol would be thrown into a furnace and burned alive. The culture-clash came to a boil when the trumpets were sounded and everyone bowed down to worship the idol, all except Shadrach, Meshach, and Abednego. Fueled by festering jealousy, the astrologers reported them to the king.

Furious with rage, Nebuchadnezzar summoned Shadrach, Meshach and Abednego. So these men were brought before the king, and Nebuchadnezzar said to them, "Is it true, Shadrach, Meshach and Abednego, that you do not serve my gods or worship the image of gold I have set up? Now when you hear the sound of the horn, flute, zither, lyre, harp, pipes and all kinds of music, if you are ready to fall down and worship the image I made, very good. But if you do not worship it, you will be thrown immediately into a blazing furnace. Then what god will be able to rescue you from my hand?"

Shadrach, Meshach and Abednego replied to the king, "O Nebuchadnezzar, we do not need to defend ourselves before you in this matter. If we are thrown into the blazing furnace, the God we serve is able to save us from it, and He will rescue us from your hand, O king. But even if He does not, we want you to know, O king, that we will not serve your gods or worship the image of gold you have set up. (Daniel 3:13-18)

The king ordered that the furnace be heated seven times as hot as usual. It was so hot that the soldiers who took the three bound men to the furnace were killed by the flames; and Shadrach, Meshach, and Abednego fell in.

That's when the story really gets interesting. As the king looked in, he saw not three, but four men, walking around in the furnace. Bible scholars tell us the fourth person was likely the pre-incarnate Christ. When Shadrach, Meshach, and Abednego came out of the furnace, they were unaffected by the fire. Their clothes didn't even smell like smoke.

God provided for His faithful servants in many ways. First, He placed the three of them together so that they could encourage and strengthen each other. He rewarded their obedience by placing them in positions of prominence. And when they needed Him, He showed up to deliver them from the flames.

In this case God revealed Himself by rescuing them from martyrdom, thus revealing His sovereignty to the Babylonians. But, sometimes He reveals Himself by providing courage, strength, and grace in the face of martyrdom, as He did for Jesus' apostles.

The common bond that ties the heroes from the days of Daniel with the martyrs of the New Testament (and those who face persecution and possible death today) was faith in the sovereignty of God. They knew that He was able to rescue them, but refused to compromise even if He chose to deliver them into His presence through a martyr's death. Their lives belonged to Him and He was free to do with them whatever best suited His sovereign purpose.

Whatever you may be facing right now, He already knows all about it. You can trust Him to be there with you and to bring the appropriate outcome. If you belong to Him, He will not leave you alone in your distress. He has the right to rule your life, and His rule is always right.

As I write this, I have prayed for all who will eventually read it. He knows your heart. He knows your need. He loves you just as you are. And He will answer when you call to Him.

Gideon was threshing wheat in a winepress to keep it from the Midianites. (Judges 6:11)

In Gideon's day, threshing wheat was usually done in an open area, as a sort of community activity. It requires space and a light wind to blow away the chaff after it's been separated from the grain.

The winepress, on the other hand tended to be a pit in a more sheltered area, often surrounded by stones, sometimes even inside a cave. Gideon was working in the winepress so as to hide himself and his grain from the enemy.

The Midianites had moved in, set up camp and every night they would sneak in and steal crops, farm animals, and the Israelites' sense of security. Midian so impoverished the Israelites that they cried out to the Lord for help.

Isn't that just like us? We spend so much time hiding from reality. All the while we allow the enemy to steal and destroy much of the good that God has poured out on us. But God speaks life and encouragement to us even while we are hiding in the winepress. *When the Angel of the Lord appeared to Gideon he said, 'The Lord is with you mighty warrior'... 'Go in the strength you have and save Israel out of Midian's hand. Am I not sending you?' 'But Lord,' Gideon replied, 'how can I save Israel? My clan is the weakest in Manasseh, and I am the least in my family'.*

Too often we, like Gideon, try to process God's truths while we are in a pit. The truth gets buried in fear and rebellion, and is never fully internalized. Like wheat that is threshed in a winepress, the chaff never blows away. It just piles up around us burying, contaminating, and obscuring the wheat; while preventing the wheat from being of real benefit or nourishment to us. Gideon totally missed the fact that it was God's strength and stature that mattered.

So it is when we try to process God's truth while we are in the valley of sin, defeat, or discouragement. Until we reach up and take God's hand so that He can lift us out of the pit – until we surrender to His Lordship – the truth of His love, His power, and His purpose never begins to nourish our souls. Victory is there all the time. But buried under the lies of the enemy, we cannot see that the way out is straight up. When God lifts us up, the gentle breath of His mercy blows Satan's lies away like the chaff.

Once Gideon understood Who was sending him everything changed. He tore down the altars to the idols the Israelites had begun to worship. He built an altar to the Lord. He raised an army of 30,000 men to drive the Midianites out of Israel's territory. He was finally on board. He knew he could win. He was ready for anything. Or so he thought.

But God had other, even bigger plans. *The Lord said to Gideon, 'You have too many men for me to deliver Midian into their hands. In order that Israel may not boast against me that her own strength has saved her.'* Do we realize that when we brag about our talents, assets, or accomplishments, we are boasting against God?

Finally, when God, through the process of elimination, had reduced the number in Gideon's army from 30,000 to 300, He brought them to where the *"Midianites, Amalekites, and all the other eastern peoples had settled in the valley, thick as locusts"*. It was an improbable battle. Gideon armed each of his 300 men with a trumpet and a jar with only a torch inside, divided them into three companies of 100 men, and moved to the edge of the enemy camp.

The 300 were obviously the most watchful, as evidenced by the way that they scooped the water up to drink it rather than lowering their faces (and their guard) to the water. But, they also must have been the most humble and faith-filled of the 30,000 who originally showed up. There's no record of anyone questioning God's instruction or grumbling about Gideon's leadership. They confidently prepared for battle.

The three companies blew the trumpets and smashed the jars. Grasping the torches in their left hands and holding in their right hands the trumpets they were to blow they shouted, 'A sword for the Lord and for Gideon!' While each man held his position around the camp, all the Midianites ran, crying out as they fled. When the 300 trumpets sounded, the Lord caused the men throughout the camp to turn on each other with their swords.

All the Israelites had to do was obey – they showed up, stood firm, proclaimed the name of the Lord, and shone the light that God gave them. They obeyed God because they trusted Him. That's exactly what God expects of us as we follow Him each day. As He did for them, He will do the rest.

All Scripture is taken from Judges 6-7

He lifted me out of the slimy pit, out of the mud and mire; He set my feet on a rock and gave me a firm place to stand. (Psalm 40:2)

When he was a teenager, our son Nathaniel, drove a 1978 white Chevy truck with a big engine that he lovingly called "White Trash". And he did love that truck. But he occasionally took it mud-bogging. We live in a rural area of southeastern Georgia and the kids around here like to take their vehicles into muddy fields where they drive in circles and splash around until their truck is covered with as much mud as will stick. This is a very bad idea.

If you leave the mud on the truck, it causes rust and decay, and not just to the body of the truck. In the heart of the truck, the engine, it clogs air filters, causes things to overheat (okay I'm not a mechanic) and to rust. It can destroy the vehicle completely. And as it covers the windshield, the mud blinds you to where you are going.

Sin is very much like mud-bogging. It can be a lot of fun, but always leaves us dirty. And the longer we remain caked with the mire of rebellion, the more damage it does. It becomes difficult to see that we are headed down the wrong road. Sin clogs our spirits with guilt, eats at our very souls and leads to the devastation of divorce, addiction, poverty, emptiness, selfishness, greed, lust, despair and death.

But, with God all things are possible. When we cry out to Him in repentance, He comes and rescues us. He lifts us up, cleans us up, forgives us, heals us, and then forgets about it. When we are done with our sin, so is He. God prefers to keep His children moving forward into ever greater forgiveness, peace, freedom and victory, He chooses to leave the past in the past.

The times that He has delivered me have become major faith builders, reminding me of the gentle faithfulness of the Father who rescues me simply because He delights in me. The joy of living in freedom inspires me to keep short accounts with God when it comes to sin. I don't want to silence the voice of the Holy Spirit so I try to respond in quick and humble repentance when He points out my words, thoughts, or behavior that offend God.

The victories that He has afforded in the past build confidence in His unconditional love. His love inspires me to want to find out just what He can do with me when I stay on the narrow Way.

It isn't an easy path to navigate, but having personally experienced the difficulties of temptation, Christ provided us with a road map and a Guide: His Word and His Holy Spirit.

Psalm 119:105 calls the Bible a lamp for my feet and a light for my path. There are no street lights where I live, and a flashlight is a very good friend to have when you're outside in the darkness. But, no matter how good they are, most hand-held lights do not illuminate large areas. They emit just enough light to keep moving forward, to safely take that next step down whatever path you're trying to navigate.

In the same way, the Holy Spirit leads us step by step. When temptation has us going in circles, He alone is able to lovingly remind us of the results of past failures, but only so that we can remember why we don't want to go there again. He gives us enough light to keep going in the right direction, but not enough to see the obstacles that might make us afraid to move forward.

Yet when we keep moving steadily forward, spending time with God each day in the Word and in prayer, the light of faith grows brighter. We begin to see more of His plan; and we see more clearly that God is clearing the obstacles on our behalf.

Then the Spirit of the Lord came upon Jahaziel son of Zechariah ...as he stood in the assembly. He said, 'Listen, King Jehoshaphat and all who live in Judah and Jerusalem. This is what the Lord says to you; 'Do not be afraid or discouraged because of this vast army. For the battle is not yours, but God's ...You will not have to fight this battle. Take up your positions; stand firm and see the deliverance the Lord will give you. ...Do not be afraid; do not be discouraged. Go out to face them tomorrow, and the Lord will be with you.'

Hundreds of years after Gideon lived, when Jehoshaphat was King of Judah, they found themselves once more under attack. Besieged by the Moabites, Ammonites and some of the Meunites, Jehoshaphat cried out to the Lord for deliverance.

As the armies of Judah prepared to march out to meet the enemy, Jehoshaphat appointed men to sing to the Lord and to praise Him for the splendor of His holiness as they went out at the head of the army, saying: 'Give thanks to the Lord, for His love endures forever'. As they began to sing and praise, the Lord set ambushes against the men of Ammon and Moab and Mount Seir who were invading Judah, and they were defeated. The men of Ammon and Moab rose up against the men from Mount Seir to destroy and annihilate them. After they finished slaughtering the men from Seir, they helped to destroy one another. When the men of Judah came to the place that overlooks the desert and looked toward the vast army, they saw only dead bodies lying on the ground; no one had escaped."

As we face daily trials, God says the same thing to us: *Do not be afraid or discouraged ...For the battle is not yours but God's. ...You will not have to fight this battle. Take up your positions; stand firm and see the deliverance the Lord will give you.*

It isn't easy to stand firm when you're under attack. I've been there and the urge is to run as far and as fast from the battle as you can possibly go. Just as God turned Israel's enemies' swords against each other, He will turn our enemy's lies and attacks back on Satan. The Bible is God's biography. As you study, you see that faithfulness is a thread that runs throughout. He is capable of doing again anything that He did in the past, and so much more.

When you do manage to stand firm, God shows up. Sometimes He uses one of His servants, a brother or sister in Christ, to defend you. Sometimes He simply scatters your enemies. Always, as He did on Calvary, He puts Himself between you and destruction. There can be no safer place to hide than in the cleft of the Rock of Ages.

One image of the 9/11 attacks that still haunts me is of the "First Responders". In the midst of chaos and unbelievable destruction, when everyone else was running as fast as possible away from the crumbling buildings, the Firefighters, Medics, and Police Officers ran toward the disaster. I remember watching as one by one they would lead someone out of harm's way, then turn and run back toward the crumbling buildings. Many sacrificing their own lives while trying to save one more person.

Jesus is the true First Responder. He responded to our helplessness and hopelessness by sacrificing Himself to rescue us from an eternity in Hell. You can trust Him. He will never fail you.

All Scripture is taken from 2 Chronicles 20

And he arose, and rebuked the wind, and said unto the sea, Peace, be still. And the wind ceased, and there was a great calm. (Mark 4:39)

Our eldest son, Brian was forced to be away from his family for an extended work assignment several months ago. The weekend that he was scheduled to depart, we visited them for some family time, grandsons' soccer games, and yet another poignant trip to the airport. As they do each night, their little family gathered for worship before tucking the boys in for the night.

Brian brought out his guitar and played as they sang each family member's favorite praise song or chorus. They read from the Bible and prayed together. I've been in many church services where the Spirit's presence was not nearly as palpable as it was that night. It has become one of my most cherished memories, the kind that a mother "treasures in her heart". Thanks to "red tape", the departure was delayed and Brian had an opportunity to record their favorite worship songs for his family to use in his physical absence.

To make the separation easier they would video chat as often as possible. Each of the children rested his head at night on a pillow case that was printed with a photo of him with his dad, and cuddled up with a little blanket that their mom kept scented with Dad's cologne. I know that my grandsons felt their daddy's love in his physical absence; and that worshiping with their father's accompaniment on his guitar had a reassuring effect on them.

My family has been through some extraordinarily difficult times over the last few years. But really the last twenty-one years of my life have read like a list of the most traumatic experiences in a woman's life - sometimes several occurring simultaneously. Many have been the times when I could not have kept going except for the tender loving care of a Savior who knows how it feels to suffer loss, rejection, and pain.

There have been a few days when Jesus' loving embrace was as palpable to me as if He were there in body, as well as Spirit. One that really stands out in my mind happened when my own father was in the last stages of lung cancer. It had been a particularly exhausting day involving a trek to the hospital for a radiation treatment in weather that was as heavy and dreary as my own heart. It was so hard watching him bravely press on even as his body began to fail him.

At the end of such days I was usually so drained and numb with grief when I got home that I was certain I would not be able to get up and do it all over again tomorrow. This had been a particularly hard day because, for the first time, I saw the light of hope fading in his eyes.

As I sat down on the edge of my bed I mindlessly turned on the TV. My television was tuned to a Christian channel that I didn't usually watch that was airing an MTV-style video program. The strain of the day began to melt away as I listened to the beautiful melody of a song by Nicole C. Mullen, *Redeemer*. It was as comforting as if Christ had been there physically embracing me.

Enveloped in His peace, I slept well that night. And for those last few weeks of my dad's life, when things got too hard for me to bear, it was as if the Holy Spirit switched on a little music player in the depths of my soul, reminding me that my Redeemer is alive, He is there, He understands, He cares, and that His strength is enough.

Whether things are going well or you find yourself caught in the middle of some storm, I heartily recommend sitting quietly with your eyes closed and listening to songs of faith. Feel yourself begin to relax as He gently comes and wraps His arms around you and whispers comfort into your soul. You might just find tension, fear, anger, self-pity, and whatever else might be gnawing at you begin to melt into joy, and that unfathomable peace that only He can give.

Be still my soul; the waves and wind still know
His voice who ruled them while He dwelt below.

--Catharine von Schlegel

Jesus did many other miraculous signs in the presence of his disciples which are not recorded in this book. But these are written that you may believe that Jesus is the Christ, the Son of God. (John 20:30-31)

Mary Did You Know? is a beautiful Christmas song written by Christian singer and comedian, Mark Lowry. He lists many of the miraculous acts of Jesus recorded in the Gospels and wonders aloud whether Mary knew all that her new baby would accomplish in His lifetime here among His creation.

I don't know whether Mary knew the details of His future, that He would walk on water, heal the sick, feed thousands, raise the dead, and be raised from the dead. But she knew His past.

Mary knew that an angel suddenly appeared to her with a message from God that she, out of all the women who ever had existed or would exist, had been chosen to bear God's child; and that God had confirmed that truth to Joseph, her beloved husband-to-be. Because Joseph not only protected her from being stoned to death, but also safeguarded her purity by not claiming the rights of a husband, she knew that she was still a virgin when her baby boy was born.

She knew that shepherds arrived on His birth day to see her baby, whose birth had been announced to them by angels. And as time passed, Mary had seen men arrive from far away to worship her little boy - their pathway illumined by a brilliant star, bearing expensive gifts with which to honor Him. Treasures that likely financed their family's flight to Egypt when His life was in danger from a jealous little king.

Mary knew that God, The Father, had provided a stepfather for his son who would listen obediently to God's voice. She had seen Joseph protect and nurture God's child and the child's mother, remaining in Egypt until Herod had died and it was safe to return to the town of Nazareth in Galilee.

Mary saw her son, Jesus, grow in knowledge so great that He was teaching the priests in the Temple in Jerusalem, God's dwelling place on earth, by the time He was twelve years old. And in John 2:1-11, the Apostle John tells us that when Jesus and Mary attended a wedding together in Cana, she already knew that He had a Creator's power.

I believe that, as God the Creator, the wine that Jesus created in the water jars was likely the juice of the perfect grape. It was newly created juice that likely tasted the way it would if it could be extracted without piercing, bruising, crushing, or fermenting the grape. John tells us that the wedding guests had never tasted anything like it.

I've always thought it such a tender thing that, as He was hanging on the cross, Jesus was concerned about His mother's future wellbeing, instructing John to take her into his home so that she would be cared for. But, Jesus had half-brothers and half-sisters who were reared by His own godly parents. I doubt that Mary would ever have been homeless.

I have come to believe that Jesus may have been providing more for John than for Mary. Perhaps Jesus sent Mary to John so that he could write with assurance the truth of the Gospel.

John needed to hear from the only eyewitness who could authenticate the deity of Christ. Only Mary could give him a first-person account of Jesus' conception, birth, and His life prior to that day when He said to John, Follow Me. John needed to know the whole story so that he could write the Gospel of John, the book that was: ...*written that you may believe that Jesus is the Messiah, the Son of God, and that by believing you may have life in His name. (John 20:31)*

"For my thoughts are not your thoughts, neither are your ways my ways", declares the Lord. "As the heavens are higher than the earth, so are my ways higher than your ways and my thoughts than your thoughts.

As the rain and the snow come down from heaven, and do not return to it without watering the earth and making it bud and flourish, so that it yields seed for the sower and bread for the eater, so is my word that goes out from my mouth:

It will not return to me empty; but will accomplish what I desire and achieve the purpose for which I sent it." (Isaiah 55:8-11)

I gained a deeper understanding of this passage a few years ago when my sister lay gravely injured in the Trauma Unit of a local hospital. She was heavily medicated with drugs for pain that are designed to cause the patient to not remember things that occur while under their influence. She was also affected by residual effects of general anesthesia used in multiple surgeries, many lasting as long as 8-10 hours and occurring as often as twice some weeks.

Reeling and in shock from the gravity of the events that had rocked the very foundations of our family, I was too numb and confused to know how to reach her in her unconscious state. I prayed for strength each time I took the long walk down the hallway to her room. As I stood by her bed, holding her hand, and quietly praying for her, I began to be prompted by the Holy Spirit to tell her that she would be okay, that she was going to make it through this. These were things that I was not sure that my mind believed, but as I said them I knew in my heart that they were true.

I told her that God was with her - strengthening her and healing her wounds. I told her how many friends and family members had come to the hospital to show their love and support for her, and that hundreds of people around the world were praying for her. She remembers all of those things, and only those things, about the first month in the hospital.

I also sang to her and told her other little newsy tidbits about family, etc. We talked during brief periods when she was awake, but the only things she recalls about my visits were those things that God had led me to say to her. While she had many visitors, she only remembers seeing our other sister, Georgia, and me. We were both saying the same things to her.

I think that what is unique about the words that are God-inspired is that they go directly to the spirit, not so much the mind. They are not always Bible verses, but will always agree with scripture, express the heart of God for a given situation, and be spoken by the Holy Spirit, through a believer, for a specific need. They can work miracles as they accomplish His purpose.

Linda told me later that it was those words, spoken by her sisters that kept her fighting when she might have been tempted to give up. As I began to believe them, they ministered as much to me as they did to her.

Gently as a spring rain they watered my soul, causing faith to grow in the fertile soil of my broken heart. God drew so near that it felt as though I could reach out and touch Him. I now know without any doubt that when you call on His name, He shows up. When you open your heart, He speaks. I hope you don't miss the magnitude of that truth. There is nothing extraordinary about me, or my sisters. But we do serve an extraordinary God.

My God turns my darkness into light. (Psalm 18:28)

These last couple of years have been a rough ride on an emotional roller coaster. There have been career changes, births, graduations, weddings, birthdays, anniversaries, and miracles. But there also have been job losses, addictions, broken relationships, adultery, abandonments, deaths, murder, jail visits, divorces, surgeries, and lengthy stays at the hospital. All within our immediate families. There has been much to rejoice over, and a darkness that I never knew existed. Pure evil entered my world and brought its dark cloak of fear, pain, and despair.

In the midst of the blackness, God shines the light of His love, grace, and mercy into a hurting heart, lifting the darkness. What a difference a simple change of perspective can make. If we focus on the sad things, the darkness can easily consume our hearts, our minds, and our very souls. So when darkness surrounds you, change your perspective. Take your eyes off the problems and take a good look at the One Who can solve them.

I am so thankful for the beauty of God's light, shone on His creation, like His mercies, brand new each day. *Because of the Lord's great love we are not consumed, for His compassions (mercies) never fail. They are new every morning; great is Your faithfulness. (Lamentations 3:22-23)*

When you are in the darkness the pupils of your eyes dilate to let in more light so that you can see better. In the same way, when we are walking in the spiritual darkness of fear, grief, loneliness, rejection, or whatever your present darkness may be, God dilates the eyes of our souls so that we can see Him there walking beside us in the darkness, clearing the pathway so that we will not stumble, shielding us from the evil that lurks in the darkness, and bearing provision for every need we will face.

The key to walking safely through the darkness is to stay close to Jesus. Hold tightly to His nail-scarred hand. He knows the way whether He put you on that path, or it was your choice, or you got there because of someone else's bad choice. He never leaves you nor forsakes you in the darkness.

He left the perfect light of Heaven to come to earth as a helpless infant. Even the sunniest days in Israel must have seemed dim compared to the light of His Father's throne room. He faced every temptation known to man without wavering in His obedience to His Father's will. Then He suffered, not only an agonizing death, but the darkness of being forsaken by God. When your sin and mine were placed on Him, God's only Son became too ugly for God even to look at. He does not just know the way through the darkness; He is the way through the darkness.

Do not fret because of evil men or be envious of those who do wrong; for like the grass they will soon wither, like green plants they will soon die away. (Psalm 37:1-2)

Dictionaries provide several definitions for the word fret: to wear away or corrode the surface of something; to create a hole in something by constant wear or rubbing; to flow with constant rippling motion or with choppy waves; to be worried, irritated, or anxious about something. Although the last one applies most directly to the context of the passage, all imply destruction or turmoil.

Chârâh, the Hebrew root for fret, means to grow warm; to blaze up in anger, jealousy, or zeal implying a blazing intensity of emotion. Whether you experience worry, guilt, anger, fear, or jealousy, when you allow them to grow into fretfulness, they can easily create turmoil in your soul like the waves of a storm, gradually wearing a hole in your faith. The result will likely be withdrawal from God, and/or withdrawal from service to your fellow man. But God says,

Trust in the Lord and do good; dwell in the land and enjoy safe pasture. Delight yourself in the Lord and He will give you the desires of your heart. (Psalm 37:3-4)

Jesus is the remedy for fretfulness. Study Him by studying, memorizing, and meditating on His Word. Worship Him through prayer and music. Find the same joy in His presence that you find with your beloved family and friends.

Commit your way to the Lord; trust in Him and He will do this: He will make your righteousness shine like the dawn, the justice of your cause like the noonday sun. (Psalm 37:5-6)

Trust Him with your heart, your reputation, your possessions, your relationships, your today, and your tomorrows. Obey His leadership and leave the outcome in His hands. Even though you may experience persecution or rejection because of obedience to Him, remain faithful. I have experienced rejection and mild persecution, but His Word, and the testimony of 2000 years of martyrs testify that He is bigger than anything man can do.

Be still before the Lord and wait patiently for Him; do not fret when men succeed in their ways, when they carry out their wicked schemes. (Psalm 37:7)

I have been through several seasons of sitting at His feet, studying, praying, and waiting. When you wait for Him to act on your behalf or to show you what to do, you will truly begin to understand the boundless provision of God.

There is nothing more humbling than to be silent and alone in distress, and to have God raise up someone to speak on your behalf; or to watch Him move in amazing ways to bring about His purpose from an impossible situation.

If you allow yourself to be consumed by fretfulness, you will allow bitterness, fear, or even hatred to take root in your soul. All of these can become strongholds of sin through which your only real enemy, Satan, will wreak havoc in every area of your life.

Refrain from anger and turn from wrath; do not fret -- it leads only to evil. For evil men will be cut off, but those who hope in the Lord will inherit the land. (Psalm 37:8-9)

Finally, trust God, delight in Him and He will bring your heart into agreement with His. Obey His direction for your life and He will fulfill His purpose in and through you.

Allow Him to deal with those who mistreat you. He may deal with them differently than you would like, but it will always be done according to His purpose for them. And you will find comfort and peace.

I have told you these things, so that in Me you may have peace. In this world you will have trouble. But take heart! I have overcome the world. (John 16:33)

Help me understand the meaning of your precepts so that I can meditate on your wonders. ...Keep me from the way of deceit and graciously give me your instruction. I have chosen the way of truth. I have set your ordinances before me. I cling to your decrees; LORD, do not put me to shame. I pursue the way of your commands for you broaden my understanding. (Psalm 119:27, 29-32)

Getting centered has become increasingly popular in the West over the last 40 years or so. With the spread of Eastern religions, especially as taught by the Maharishi Mahesh Yogi, Transcendental Meditation (TM) has been popularized by celebrities, karate and yoga instructors, psychologists, and life coaches alike. You choose a word on which to focus (your mantra), then you sit quietly for 15 to 20 minutes focusing all your mental and spiritual energy on an area just below your navel, which is believed to be your "place of knowingness". It's true; I could not make this stuff up. TM is all about reaching a level of peace, love, happiness, contentment, or emptiness from the craziness of life. But are you not really just becoming "self" centered?

TM is supposed to create confidence in you that will lead to success. But is it not just another of Satan's lies? The Bible tells us, *Be strong and courageous. Be careful to obey all the law my servant Moses gave to you; do not turn from it to the right or to the left, that you may be successful wherever you go. Keep this book of the law always on your lips; meditate on it day and night, so that you may be careful to do everything written in it. Then you will be prosperous and successful. (Joshua 1:8)*

Even if you were to choose "Jesus" as your mantra, unless you went beyond the word to the resurrected savior, the One who was given that name in a cold stable more than two millennia ago, it still would be a meaningless exercise. It isn't merely a word on which we are to meditate, it's The Word of God: alive, active, and sharper than a two-edged sword. God speaks to us through His Word, revealing His character, His plans, His purpose, and His love. In short, He gets my focus off of myself and fully onto Him where it belongs. Psalm 119:11 says, *I have treasured your Word in my heart so that I may not sin against you.*

Being centered around anything temporal and changing often leaves us as easily distracted as the average three-year-old, drifting from "ism" to "ism" like so much chaff in the wind. Rather, the Word says,

Blessed is the one who does not walk in step with the wicked or stand in the way that sinners take, or sit in the company of mockers, but whose delight is in the law of the Lord, and who meditates on His law day and night.

That person is like a tree planted by streams of water, which yields its fruit in season, and whose leaf does not wither -- and whatever they do prospers.

Not so the wicked! they are like chaff that the wind blows away. Therefore the wicked will not stand in the judgment, nor sinners in the assembly of the righteous. For the Lord watches over the way of the righteous; but the way of the wicked leads to destruction. (Psalm 1)

It matters how and with whom I spend my time. It matters what kind of language I use and whether I conduct myself with integrity. It matters how I think and on whom or what I meditate. Character is determined by those things that I pour into myself. And if I claim the name of Christ, my character reflects on Him in the eyes of a world that does not know Him.

My husband was, for many years, a computer programmer. One of their many little catchphrases was summed up as GIGO, or Garbage In = Garbage Out. If they programmed the computer with the wrong information and commands, they got useless results.

How much more important is what I put into my heart, soul, and spirit. If I feed on God's Word, spend time communicating with Him through prayer, obey His written Word and the promptings of His Holy Spirit within me, I will become a useful vessel in His hands. When I surrendered myself to Him, I became a new creation -- a child of the Living God. But, am I living like what I have become?

Have I not commanded you? Be strong and courageous. Do not be afraid, do not be discouraged; for the Lord your God will be with you wherever you go. (Psalm 46:8-9)

Set your mind on things above, not on earthly things. For you died, and your life is now hidden with Christ in God. Put to death, therefore, whatever belongs to your earthly nature: sexual immorality, impurity, lust, evil desires, and greed which is idolatry. Because of these, the wrath of God is coming. You used to walk in these ways, in the life you once lived. But now you must rid yourself of all such things as these: anger, rage, malice, slander, and filthy language from your lips. ...Therefore, as God's chosen people, holy and dearly loved, clothe yourselves with compassion, kindness, humility, gentleness, and patience. (Colossians 3:2-8)

It is a fearsome thing to be called by the name of God. We nonchalantly call ourselves "Christians" - followers of Christ. But, do the people who see us on Monday through Saturday have any idea who the Christ of Christianity is?

What does the person who saw you drink too much and behave foolishly or seductively at the bar or the party on Friday night think of Him when they see you singing in the choir or teaching Sunday School, if they happen to visit your church?

What does your server at the restaurant think of Him after you leave? Do you pray publicly, then complain loudly about service and stiff the server on the tip before you leave? Or, do you bless them with kind words and a generous tip regardless of their job performance? Do you live as if someone else's bad behavior justifies your own?

The same principle applies to every area of your life. How do you treat slow cashiers, bad drivers, sales clerks, the maid who cleans your hotel room, or the thuggish-looking kid loitering at the mall? What do they think of Him after they encounter you?

We often act as if we're being horribly inconvenienced by God's ownership of us. We become offended by the debt of gratitude that is revealed in the Word of God, as if we deserved the unfathomable gift of redemption that was given to us. But the truth is that God made us, He paid the price for our sin, and He has the right to direct our lives. He is Creator of all, and He is LORD of all - whether you like it or not.

When I was a child it used to be quite popular to make a statement of belief, in unison, as a church body. One frequently quoted statement was, "God said it. I believe it. That settles it." That always bothered me. I felt (and still do) the last two sentences are out or order. The truth is that if God said it, then that settles it, whether I believe it or not.

Some things are true whether you and I believe them or not. If God says something, it is true. He is God. He gets to make the rules. How well I obey Him will dictate how effective my testimony about Him will be.

I have often heard it said that hypocritical Christians are the leading cause of atheism in the world. But, like everyone else, Christians are flawed human beings. We can't possibly live out our faith perfectly. The hard-hearted just use our seeming hypocrisy as an excuse for their rebellion.

The point is that we allow God, through His Spirit, to direct our minutes. It's easy to justify "mistakes" if we think of following Christ as a life-long goal, rather than a total surrender of ourselves – mind, will, emotions, body, abilities, possessions, and rights – to His perfect will and direction. It's a mistake to believe that you always have time to repent and get it right later when you have finished enjoying your sin.

A big part of growing in Christ is breaking the habit of living as you have in the past and developing the habit of following Him. If you wait until you "feel like a Christian" to begin to live like one, you will be forever in the wilderness. Begin to live up to what you know about Him. Open your heart when you open His Word. Learn from Him what He expects of His followers. Pray your way through the day and you will find the power to live up to His expectations, along with the mercy to start over again tomorrow. He knows the heart of every person you will encounter along the way; and He knows the need that He may have planned for you to meet.

It's amazing how effectively He uses the time that you spend with Him each day to change you into the person you committed to be at your conversion.

Why, my soul are you downcast? Why so disturbed within me? Put your hope in God, for I will yet praise Him, my Savior and my God. (Psalm 43:5)

*C*he Book of Psalms is a collection of poetry and hymns in the heart of the Bible. The Psalms speak deeply to me about the common nature of human experience throughout the ages. Although the book is generally attributed to King David, scholars believe it was written by a number of poets and musicians over an extended period of time.

But Psalm 43 certainly seems to fit into the scheme of David's life as he was being pursued by Saul. Whoever authored Psalm 43, obviously was persecuted, alone, afraid, and suffering: *Vindicate me, O God, and plead my cause against an ungodly nation; rescue me from deceitful and wicked men. (vs. 1)*

He was so alone that he even felt rejected by God, but also knew that only God could rescue him from his trouble: *You are God my stronghold. Why have you rejected me? Why must I go about mourning, oppressed by the enemy? Send forth your light and your truth, let them guide me; let them bring me to your holy mountain, to the place where you dwell. Then will I go to the altar of God, to God, my joy and my delight. I will praise you with the harp, O God, my God. (vs. 2-4)*

The Psalmist was hunkered down somewhere - alone, depressed, withdrawn from his friends, and hiding from his foes. He was isolated (perhaps by choice) from the company of anyone who could encourage him to seek after God, or even worship God with him.

I have been in that dark place many times. I don't know who his physical enemies were. But at the heart of isolation from God we all have a common enemy, Satan. He smiles when a child of God pulls away from God and His people. He rejoices when she chooses to put down roots in the desolate garden of loneliness; at that moment, she has become his prisoner.

But there is a cure for such spiritual sickness. As the Psalmist's focus began to change so did his attitude. Rather than worrying about his problems, whining about his situation, and longing for change, he began to change his thinking.

He encouraged himself by focusing on who God is. He began to see light and hope. He remembered the joy and delight of past intimacy with God, times spent singing praises to God.

I tend to talk to myself, so I relate to his self-questioning. I usually ask myself, "Why are you sitting here meditating on all this negative stuff?" Or, "Is this really the best use of your time and brain cells?" Not as poetic as the Psalmist's questions, but the gist is the same. And he found the same solution to his problems that I always find:

Do you not know? Have you not Heard? The Lord is the everlasting God, the Creator of the ends of the earth. He will not grow tired or weary, and His understanding no one can fathom. He gives strength to the weary, and increases the power of the weak. Even youths grow tired and weary, and young men stumble and fall; but those who hope in the Lord will renew their strength. They will soar on wings like eagles; they will run and not grow weary, they will walk and not be faint. (Isaiah 40:28-31)

*Reflect upon your present
blessings, of which every man
has many—not on your past
misfortunes, of which all men
have some.*

- Charles Dickens

Part Four

But we never can prove
The delights of His love,
Until all on the altar we lay;
For the favor He shows,
And the joy He bestows,
Are for them who will trust and obey.

So do not fear, for I am with you; do not be dismayed, for I am your God. I will strengthen you and help you; I will uphold you with my righteous right hand. (Isaiah 41:10)

From my journal: May 28, 2009. What a day. A grand Jury indicted my nephew on two counts of murder, one count of aggravated battery, and a number of other charges in the attack on his family.

It's funny I still can close my eyes and see the adorable little boy with red curls, wearing a blue suit that nearly matched his eyes, peering suspiciously at my husband as he removed my garter at our wedding reception. He was my "first" little boy. I was only fourteen when he was born to my sister Linda and her husband Philip. Can there be any greater joy for a teen-aged girl than a "living doll" to play with? I loved babysitting him. He even went on dates with Jimmy and me before we married. So it was appropriate that he was there at that special moment.

Now, he stands accused of killing his father and youngest brother, and trying to kill his mother, my sister. It is nearly impossible for me to accept even the possibility that he might be guilty of these things. I will never understand how it came to this, but here we are.

And so, today I took Grant outside to do our regular check on the vegetable and flower gardens. You have never really seen the world until you see it through the eyes of a highly curious two-year-old boy. Everything is an adventure; they never wonder about motives or the possibility of evil and hatred in the world.

To Grant the world is a wonderful place to explore. So when a rather small Monarch butterfly landed on one of the lavender plants that flank the archway leading to my front walk, he thought nothing of just reaching over and gently touching it, just another colorful creature to investigate.

Then the truly amazing thing happened, the butterfly didn't escape when Grant withdrew his hand. It sat there as if waiting for another touch, which Grant happily supplied. I watched in wonder as Grant gently caressed the butterfly with the tiny index finger of his left hand. The entire encounter lasted only a few seconds. The butterfly floated away on a soft breeze toward the petunias on the other side of the path. Grant moved on to the next adventure, never realizing what a rare encounter he'd just experienced.

It was much later that evening, after Grant had gone home and the house was very still, as I sat alone and thought back to the fragile beauty of that remarkable moment between boy and butterfly, I heard the Spirit gently whisper to my soul, "That was for you."

As I pondered the encounter I realized how much it mirrors our relationship with our heavenly Father. He possesses the power to crush us with but a thought or a word, yet He reaches out to gently touch us. Is that what Grant's meeting with the butterfly was, God's gentle touch on my broken and bleeding heart? His way of saying, I am here and I see you. It may seem like a small thing, but it was more than sufficient for that dark day.

The LORD says: "These people come near to me with their mouths and honor me with their lips, but their hearts are far from me. Their worship of me is based on merely human rules they have been taught. Therefore, once more I will astound these people with wonder upon wonder; the wisdom of the wise will perish, the intelligence of the intelligent will vanish." (Isaiah 29:13-14)

The Me Generation is a phrase that was originally coined to describe my generation, also known as Baby Boomers. Born into the joyous relief of post-war America, we were something of a symbol of our parents' hope for a better tomorrow.

Having lived through the Great Depression and at least one, many of them two, World Wars they were determined to lavish us with a future filled with happiness and prosperity. Even those of us who were less wealthy by American standards were reminded how rich we were by world standards. We were assured that we could grow up to be anything we wanted. No goal was too lofty; we were the hope for tomorrow. Sadly, we came to believe our press, and became a very success-oriented, and self-centered generation.

This self-absorption has poured over into our relationships with God. As many wives remained in the paid, post-war workforce, we became the first latch-key generation. Even many of us who were raised by godly parents were led astray by the combination of lack of supervision, available media, and ubiquitous pleasure. These were not necessarily bad things in and of themselves, but together they added up to one of the fastest moral declines in human history. In one quick generation we went from a God-honoring people to adopting a rebellious, counter-culture mindset where nothing is sacred and God is no longer thought relevant.

Our reasons for rejecting Him are as varied as they are nonsensical. We may be afraid of the changes He might make in our lives. Or perhaps we just don't want anyone telling us what to do. We live as though we were complete within ourselves and smarter than Almighty God. We treat God as if He were too blind to see, or too stupid to understand, what is important. Nothing in all creation is smarter than its Creator.

Woe to those who go to great depths to hide their plans from the Lord, who do their work in darkness and think, "Who sees us? Who will know?" You turn things upside down as if the potter were thought to be like the clay! Shall what is formed say to the One who formed it, "You did not make me"? Can the pot say to the potter, "You know nothing?" (vv. 15-16)

Imagine a lump of clay crouched under the wheel trying to hide from the potter. Or picture it twisting and turning in His hands, refusing to yield to his planned designed. Or it might thrash about in the furnace, trying to escape. Your final product would be a sorely deformed pot, a broken or maybe cracked pot, or just a dried-out useless lump of clay. It seems preposterous, almost humorous. But isn't that how we treat God when we choose to live in rebellion?

There is a better way. *This is what the Sovereign Lord, the Holy One of Israel says: "In repentance and rest is your salvation, in quietness and trust is your strength, but you would have none of it. Yet the Lord longs to be gracious to you; therefore He will rise up to show you compassion. For the Lord is a God of justice. Blessed are all who wait for Him. (Isaiah 30:15, 18).*

The potter takes the lump of clay in his hands, wets it, and kneads it until it becomes pliable. The more supple the clay, the less kneading is required. He positions it firmly on the wheel and gently shapes it until it fits perfectly into his plan for it. He carefully keeps the wheel moving until the pot takes shape. He gingerly places it in the furnace to strengthen the pot and secure its shape.

In the same way, God takes us in His hands and makes of us vessels that are fitted to His plan. He kneads us with the fortifying truth of His Word. He gently shapes us through circumstances, other people, prayer, and the quiet voice of the Holy Spirit. The more teachable we are, the more perfectly we will fit His design. He purifies us in the fires of hardship and suffering to strengthen our souls with the resolve of unshakable faith. And as He did with Shadrach, Meshach, and Abednego, He walks through the furnace with us, bringing us safely through the fire to victory. He is not forming us only to fulfill His earthly plan, but also to live with Him eternally.

For what we preach is not ourselves, but Jesus Christ as Lord and ourselves as your servants for Jesus' sake. For God, who said, "Let light shine out of darkness", made His light shine in our hearts to give us the light of the knowledge of God's glory displayed in the face of Christ. But we have this treasure in jars of clay to show that this all-surpassing power is from God and not from us. So we fix our eyes not on what is seen, but on what is unseen, since what is seen is temporary, but what is unseen is eternal. (2 Corinthians 4:5-7, 18)

A farmer went out to sow his seed. As he was scattering the seed, some fell along the path; it was trampled on, and the birds of the air ate it up. Some fell on rock, and when it came up, the plants withered because they had no moisture. Other seed fell among thorns, which grew up with it and choked the plants. Still other seed fell on good soil. It came up and yielded a crop, a hundred times more than was sown.

...The seed is the word of God. Those along the path are the ones who hear, and then the devil comes and takes away the word from their hearts, so that they may not believe and be saved. Those on the rock are the ones who receive the word with joy when they hear it, but they have no root. They believe for a while, but in the time of testing they fall away. The seed that fell among the thorns stands for those who hear, but as they go on their way they are choked by life's worries, riches, and pleasures, and they do not mature. But the seed on good soil stands for those with a noble and good heart, who hear the word, retain it, and by persevering produce a crop." (Luke 8:5-8, 11-15)

In the parable of the sower, Jesus likened sharing the Word of God to sowing seeds. The ground where the Word falls is the human heart. In describing the soil in which His Word doesn't thrive, Jesus gives us a perfect picture of the attributes needed for us to believe, grow, and become fruitful members of His body.

A Truthful Heart. Those along the path who hear the truth, but allow the devil to come and steal the truth from them are self-deceived. They see themselves as just fine without God and so deceive themselves. You must be honest with yourself about your hopeless condition as a sinner in need of a Savior. *For the wages of sin is death, but the gift of God is eternal life in Christ Jesus our Lord. (Romans 6:23)*

A Tender Heart. Those whose hearts remain hard toward God never really allow Grace to sink in. They miss the truth of their hopeless condition and the fact that God sacrificed the One He holds dearest in order to make a way out of their need and into relationship with God.

The truth makes it into their heads, but never permeates their hearts and souls; so at the first sign of trouble or temptation, it withers and dies. *But God demonstrates His own love for us in this: While we were still sinners, Christ died for us. (Romans 5:8)*

A Trusting Heart. Those who fall among thorns never truly "Surrender All" to God. They still want to live their lives as they choose. They don't trust God with their time, money, resources, abilities, etc. They think it all belongs to them alone and reserve to themselves the right to do as they please.

Never fully understanding who God is, they live as if there is no God. They are driven by social norms or public opinion, and their lives look no different than if they had never heard the truth. They are immature and have little or no faith. They never truly see, much less follow, His plan for them. For it is by grace you have been saved, through faith - and this not from yourselves, it is the gift of God - not by works, so that no one can boast. (Ephesians 2:8-9)

A Triumphant Heart. Those whose hearts are good soil are those who understand their sinful condition, allow God's Grace to flood the depths of their hearts, and surrender themselves totally to His Lordship and His care. They surrender their sin and rebellion in exchange for the righteousness of Christ.

Jesus describes their hearts as noble and good. They understand that the only good and noble thing about them is that Jesus dwells within their hearts. They follow Him because they understand and desire His goodness. He produces within them His character. They share His love with those around them, and produce a crop of other believers who do the same.

I am the vine; you are the branches. If a man remains in Me and I in him, he will bear much fruit; apart from Me you can do nothing. (John 15:5)

I write these things to you who believe in the name of the Son of God so that you may know that you have eternal life. (1 John 5:13)

But He said to me, "My grace is sufficient for you, for my power is made perfect in weakness." Therefore I will boast all the more gladly about my weaknesses so that Christ's power may rest on me. (2 Corinthians 12:9)

In the course of renovating our century-old farm house, I have developed some unusual hobbies. Several years ago I discovered power tools and the joy of building things with wood. It has been a passionate love-hate relationship ever since. I've built an 8-foot-long harvest table for my kitchen, work benches for my grandsons, a doll cradle for my granddaughter, and an assortment of other items.

Last year, as I was putting the finishing touches on Corn Hole Game boards for my kids, I tore the rotator cuff in my right shoulder. It was two days before Christmas, and there were gifts to wrap, guestrooms to prepare, food to cook, etc. Since there was so much to do (and I had leftover prescription pain meds on hand and a high tolerance for pain), I didn't see a doctor until three weeks later. In the interim I probably did even greater damage to my shoulder.

I know that pain should never be ignored; it exists to tell us that something is wrong. But too often we reach for something to ease the pain without realizing the severity of the damage that is causing the pain. If the problem is minor it may heal on its own; but if the damage is serious, the best-case scenario is that we delay healing, the worst-case is that we do further damage. Rather than simple rest and physical therapy, we may require surgery.

This cycle of denial is as common when the problem is spiritual or emotional as when it's physical. I will not enter the debate on the pros and cons of antidepressants, etc. I've seen first-hand how beneficial they can be short-term in the midst of a crisis, and wouldn't presume to tell anyone what medications they should or should not take. That's an issue to be worked out between a patient and his/her health-care provider.

However, I wonder whether there might be less long-term depression if there was less dependence on medication to chase away the blues. As with physical illness or injury, emotional or mental distress is a symptom. If we simply numb the pain, rather than rooting out the source of the pain, we may never find healing. Whether the "drug" of choice is a pill, alcohol, pornography, or overwork, it is at best a temporary fix.

God designed the human body to send signals to the brain when there is pain, illness, stress, or imminent danger so that we will seek the necessary help, shelter, or rest. In the same way, He designed the human soul to seek Him in times of distress.

Biblically sound counselling with a Christian therapist, combined with Bible study and prayer, can bring healing in the most desperate of situations. Psychology and psychiatry can help you identify the source of your problems and issues. They can even help you understand the scars. But only Christ can heal your wounds; only He can safely remove the scar tissue without making more scars. Suffering brings us to the one whose suffering purchased our healing. And it is in the midst of suffering that we truly grow as a believer. As poet Robert Browning Harrison wrote:

> *I walked a mile with Pleasure; she chatted all the way.*
> *But left me none the wiser, with all she had to say.*
> *I walked a mile with Sorrow; and ne'er a word said she.*
> *But oh! The things I learned from her, when Sorrow walked with me.*

In 2 Corinthians 12, Paul wrote of a chronic problem that he described as a *thorn in my side*. He never explained whether it was a physical ailment, annoying coworker, persecutor, mental or emotional problem, or even spiritual attacks. I'm sure it's no accident that he wasn't more specific; he likely wanted his readers to know that God is sufficient for every need.

Anything that the Father allows in the life of one of His children is always for our own good, or maybe someone else's. He understands suffering better than we ever could; and He genuinely cares. Our suffering is very precious to Him. It is during times of suffering that we grow more like Him. Whatever you may be going through, HE IS BIGGER. He guides and directs the paths of our lives even when we can't see what He's doing.

He loves you more fervently than you can imagine. As Jesus showed us at Lazarus' tomb, He weeps when we weep. Psalm 56 tells us that He keeps a record of our tears and even saves them in a bottle. He cares about our suffering; and as He also showed us, He can heal anything - even death.

And onto those things that He chooses not to heal, He lavishes His grace, His strength, and His power to enable us to conquer or to persevere.

That is why, for Christ's sake, I delight in weaknesses, in insults, in hardships, in persecutions, in difficulties. For when I am weak, then I am strong. (2 Corinthians 12:10)

Come...let us walk in the light of the Lord. (Isaiah 2:5)

Ever since I was a little girl I have loved the sky. I am fascinated by clouds, stars, and even the way the blue of the sky changes as atmospheric conditions change. The sky has always been my celestial kaleidoscope.

But my favorite times to sit and look at the sky are early morning and early evening. Sunsets are beautiful, as the brilliant colors melt into each other and gradually fade into the darkness. But, I prefer a beautiful sunrise with the promise of hope for the new day.

One quality that sunrise and sunset share is the perspective they present. If you face the rising or setting sun, the world is bright, warm, and beautiful. If you turn your back to the light source, regardless of the beauty that may surround you, there is darkness.

I've found in my relationship with God that perspective and focus are everything. Whenever I turn away from Him the darkness begins to creep in. The farther away I turn the darker it becomes until the world begins to feel cold and frightening.

I'm reminded of the story I heard of a Native American boy enduring a tribal rite of passage into manhood. The men of the tribe led him into the forest on a very dark night. They drew a circle in the dirt of the forest floor and told him that he must stay in the circle all night long. The men returned to the village. As he watched the light of the torches grow faint, so did his heart.

The boy's dread increased as he listened to the howls of distant wolves, rustling of leaves, screeches and hoots of night birds, and the pounding of his own heart. Finally, weary with terror, he curled up in a ball and slipped into fitful and sporadic naps until the first little glimmer of sunrise brought startled relief.

Slowly he stretched his legs that had been almost paralyzed with fear, and as he got to his feet he caught sight of something at the edge of the little clearing, a short distance away. It was his father, who had kept silent watch over him all night, bow and arrow at the ready.

Like the boy, I often imagine myself all alone in my troubles. I worry and fret and allow the circumstances of life to all but paralyze me. But God is still there. He hasn't left me or abandoned me. His love still surrounds me. But the choice I make at that moment determines whether I will spend days, weeks, or months wandering in the darkness, or turn back toward the light of His love and the warmth of His loving embrace. By His Grace, and no small amount of His discipline, I've learned to run quickly back into His arms.

Sadness and darkness are prevalent in this fallen world. God has gently and powerfully walked me through things over the course of these last few years that I never imagined could enter into my quiet little world. Walking through the valleys with Him, my faith has grown. I have learned to trust Him more fully. And I know that nothing is too hard for Him.

So right now if you're hurting, if the darkness is creeping in or has already engulfed you, just turn around and face the light of His love. Feel the warmth of His Glory flooding over your aching heart. Take hope in the truth that the Creator knows and understands your grief. You can trust Him. He walked through the valley of the shadow of death on the way to a cross of crucifixion, so that you would see that there is life and light and joy in Him.

They are to lay their hand on the head of the sin offering and slaughter it at the place of the burnt offering. (Leviticus 4:29)

I try to read the entire Bible each year. This year I'm reading it in chronological order. I have really learned a lot. I was surprised to learn that Job apparently was a contemporary of Abraham, as his story is placed chronologically between Genesis 11 and 12. I heartily recommend putting the Bible in historical context at least once in your lifetime. I don't know why I've never done this before.

As I write this, I've just finished reading Leviticus which is undoubtedly one of the bloodier pieces of ancient literature out there. It's the story of when God literally laid down the law to the Israelites in the wilderness following their Exodus from Egypt. The first seven chapters deal with the various offerings. I would not have enjoyed the priestly duties surrounding slaughtering the animals brought as offerings, and sorting the various organs, blood, and fat. It details exactly the use or disposal of each piece of the offered animal.

When someone sinned, even unintentionally, they were required to bring a "sin offering" to make atonement for their offense against God. With this particular offering the sinner laid his hand on the animal's head symbolically transferring his sin onto the offering's head, an image used throughout the Bible. He then personally slaughtered the animal and presented it to the priest to be offered on the altar before the Lord. The sinner literally had the blood of the sacrificial animal on his hands. What a profound illustration of the flawless Sacrifice who was to come.

As Pilate held court to decide Christ's fate, he tried to avoid the execution of an innocent man. His effort was probably less a matter of conscience than his desire to avoid controversy. As Pilate "washed his hands" of the decision, *All the people answered, "His blood is on us and on our children". (Matthew 27:25)*

Every sin that you and I have committed, or ever will commit, was placed on Jesus' perfect head with that thorny crown of sin and shame. His blood is on our hands. Having been sacrificed on the Cross for my sin, in His mercy He replaces my crown of sin with His crown of righteousness.

Now there is in store for me a crown of righteousness, which the Lord, the righteous Judge, will award to me on that day - and not only to me, but also to all who have longed for His appearing. (2 Timothy 4:8)

Do not let any unwholesome talk come out of your mouths, but only what is helpful for building others up according to their needs, that it may benefit those who listen. And do not grieve the Holy Spirit of God, with whom you were sealed for the day of redemption. Get rid of all bitterness, rage and anger, brawling and slander, along with every form of malice. Be kind and compassionate to one another, forgiving each other, just as in Christ God forgave you. (Ephesians 4:29-32)

I have heard it said that bitterness is like drinking poison and expecting your enemy to die. It corrupts mind, body, and soul - eating away at your peace, your hope, and your joy. It consumes your thoughts and can lead to spiritual, physical, and mental illness. Bitterness is especially devastating when you see the one who has harmed you seeming to prosper despite the devastation they have caused in your life, and the lives of others. Every new wound seems to bring with it new scars.

Scar tissue is usually quite tough. It doesn't stretch or move the way skin and muscle are intended to function. When scars are stretched they tear, which produces new scars on top of old scars. Bitterness produces a constant meditating on the past that keeps old scars torn and bleeding. The pain produces a desire to see those who have caused our pain suffer along with us.

But God is sovereign. He reserves to Himself the right to decide what, if any, punishment is appropriate in any given situation. He also reserves the right to decide what blessing He will bestow on His children. So why does He allow them to continue to prosper when you are suffering? Only He can answer the "why" questions of life. Yet the very heart of sovereignty is that He doesn't have to answer to anyone for anything.

However, I believe that He shows great mercy in requiring us to forgive those who harm us even if He chooses to do nothing to change them, or our situation. The foundation of the forgiveness that He requires of His child is that you give up the right to seek retribution. You surrender to God alone the decision of whether to punish or bless that person. No questions asked.

If you see your enemy punished or destroyed before you have forgiven them, you might never find healing from the hurt that they've caused. The scars that remain often harden into either hopelessness or self-righteousness; both equally devastating to your future.

God's primary concern is always the condition of the heart of His child. He wants to set you free from the toxic effects of sin, both the guilt of sin to condemn us and the power of sin to control us.

When you hold on to bitterness or pain, you drag the past into your future. It's a burden you were never intended to carry. Jesus wants to carry our burdens for us so that we can once more experience the joy of belonging to Him. He desires your freedom to worship Him and to minister compassionately in His Name.

Once He has brought you to repentance and spiritual wholeness, He is then free to work His will in the life and heart of the one whom you once hated.

It is for freedom that Christ has set us free. Stand firm then, and do not let yourselves be burdened again by the yoke of slavery. (Galatians 5:1)

Teach me, LORD, the way of your decrees, that I may follow it to the end. Give me understanding, so that I may keep your law and obey it with all my heart. (Psalm 119:33-34)

Among the most common reasons I've heard from people who do not study God's Word is that it's confusing. They just don't understand it. I'm sure Satan loves to hear people express aloud the lies he has whispered in their ears for so long. But this is not how God intended it to be. He gave His Word so that we would know and understand Him. It's an autobiography, not a mystery.

I have been encouraging a friend of mine, who has gone through a lot of struggles, to spend time with God each day; not just talking to Him, but hearing from Him. The primary way that God speaks to His people is through the Bible so I urged her to try, even though she felt she couldn't understand what it was saying.

I have for years begun my day with the date-corresponding chapter from the book of Proverbs. Since there are 31 chapters it was likely designed for that purpose. It is brimming with wisdom and common-sense guidance for everyday life. I suggested that my friend give it a try.

Since she doubted her ability to understand what she would read, I told her to pray and ask God to help her understand. She did and has been on a wonderful adventure in God's Word ever since. She finished Proverbs the first couple of days and called to tell me how wonderful the Book is.

She was reading Proverbs with her young son whose spiritual training has been inconsistent at best. One morning as she was driving him to school, he was reading that day's chapter of Proverbs aloud to her in the car. He stopped and commented on a word that is at the upper edge of his vocabulary level, but he understood the context within the verse.

No one had ever told him the lie that the Bible might be confusing or hard to understand, he just got it. It's that innocence and openness to God, and His Word, that Jesus was describing when He said, *Truly, I tell you, unless you change and become like little children, you will never enter the Kingdom of Heaven. (Matthew 18:3).*

It is so wonderful to see a youngster in the faith get so excited about God's Word that she could hardly put it down, even to attend to the necessary things of life. She called later to tell me just how good God is. She had gotten a bit bogged down in the book of Exodus. She'd spent several days pondering it, not really able to get past a specific passage.

She was excited because the guest speaker at her church that day had preached from that passage; and he had illuminated the particular point that had temporarily stalled her quest to read the WHOLE Bible.

I am sure there was something in that sermon for every person in that service. And I am equally certain that the sermon was inspired, prepared, and presented on that day so that this one young woman would know that God is speaking to her, each day, through His Word.

As He has done throughout the whole of history, He still gives understanding to anyone who will just ask.

I am the light of the world. Whoever follows me will never walk in darkness, but will have the light of life. (John 8:12)

As Jesus looked up, He saw the rich putting their gifts into the temple treasury. He also saw a poor widow put in two very small copper coins. "Truly I tell you," He said, "this poor widow has put in more than all the others. All these people gave their gifts out of their wealth; but she out of her poverty put in all she had to live on." (Luke 21:1-4)

I don't believe that any encounter with Christ happens by accident. I think He probably went to the Temple on that day because there was a lesson for His followers to learn from a humble widowed woman whom He held in high esteem. A servant who obeyed Him, as she likely had for a very long time, and gave Him all that she had to live on.

Had she not already given all of herself to God it's doubtful that she would have trusted Him with the last of her resources for survival. In giving Him all her money she put feet to the claim that He was the source of all her provision, up to and including her very life. Knowing the faithfulness of our God, I doubt that she went home and starved to death. I don't imagine that she won some ancient lottery either. She was storing up treasure in Heaven where moth and rust do not destroy.

We don't know why she gave as she did. We aren't told whether she was young or old, nor whether she had children. She may have been a bit apprehensive, but I expect that what showed on her face was the joy of knowing that God was pleased with her gift. She likely went home and lived the rest of her days as she'd lived that one day when the God who had always seen her came in the flesh to show her off to His followers. Like the woman who anointed Jesus with perfume (Matthew 26:6-13), this woman's faithfulness and sacrifice will be remembered. Just as He honored her with His presence, by including her in His Story, He honors her throughout time.

Giving isn't about money; it's about priorities. God doesn't need anything from us. He is complete within Himself. Bringing our tithes and offerings to Him is about learning to trust Him with all that we have, with all that we are. Bringing the first fruits of our labor and laying it on His altar reminds us that it all comes from Him, and that it all belongs to Him.

The talents and abilities that qualify us to earn a living come from Him. The opportunities to earn a living come from Him. The favor to be successful within our chosen career comes from Him. He wants us to remember that He made us, He equipped us, and He provides for us. As long as we continue to believe that, "I earned it so it's mine to do with as I please", we will never understand the joy of living in full fellowship with God.

And even though He knows what we need even before we ask, God wants to hear us ask so that we will remember that He is the one who is meeting our needs and giving us the things we desire. Just as we want our children to come to us for the things they want and need, God wants to hear from His children.

Our giving is one of the purest indicators of our priorities. God will never direct us to give a widow's mite on an executive's salary. He wants us to be generous with the blessings that He lavishes on us. And in (Malachi 3:10), He makes a promise: Bring the whole tithe into the storehouse, that there may be food in my house. "Test me in this," says the LORD Almighty, "and see if I will not throw open the floodgates of heaven and pour out so much blessing that there will not be room enough to store it".

The evangelists of prosperity use this verse to make people believe that giving to their ministry will make you healthy, rich and good-looking. Sometimes God does pour out financial blessing, but His first priority will always be the condition of our souls. His desire is to draw us into greater intimacy with Him. He's reshaping us to be more like our Savior.

God is no fool. And it would be foolish indeed to populate heaven with greedy, manipulative people whose main objective is to show off "their" wealth. This life is but a heartbeat compared to eternity. The only wealth that you hold onto is that which you entrust to God's keeping

Give as He leads you, and rejoice in the blessings that He pours into your life. Don't be surprised to see every genuine need met, as well as those wants that fall within His will for you. More importantly, you will gain greater intimacy with Him and a deeper awareness of His active participation in every area of your life. That's something that no amount of money can buy.

The word of the Lord came to me, saying, "Before I formed you in the womb I knew you, before you were born I set you apart; I appointed you as a prophet to the nations."

"Alas, Sovereign Lord," I said, "I do not know how to speak; I am too young."

But the Lord said to me, "Do not say, 'I am too young.' You must go to everyone I send you to and say whatever I command you. Do not be afraid of them, for I am with you and will rescue you," declares the Lord. (Jeremiah 1:4-8)

I heard of a young Muslim man, who lives in the Middle East and was trying to convert a foreign friend to Islam. Unable to answer his friend's questions about Islam, in frustration he asked God to show him the truth. The LORD revealed himself in a vision, and the young man accepted Jesus as his Savior. When the new believer told his best friend what he was studying in the Bible, he too became a follower of Christ. When they shared their new faith with another friend, he also became a Christian and the three young men began to study the Bible together. What began as "evangelism" for the cause of Islam, became the birth of a new church.

Whenever Truth is sincerely sought, it is Jehovah who reveals Himself -- not Allah, Buddha, Rama, or any of the other false gods that are worshiped worldwide. Nor is it Philosophy -- Humanism, Existentialism, Marxism, or any of the other "isms" that emerged in the 19th and 20th Centuries. It doesn't matter whom the seeker thinks he is addressing, only Jehovah can reveal Truth because only He is Truth. As Jesus said, *I am the Way and the Truth and the Life. No one comes to the Father except through me. (John 14:6).*

I've never prayed for truth that I didn't receive. I believe God always answers that plea with a resounding "Yes". It is His character and His desire for us to know Truth. So it comes as no surprise that when the young Muslim man prayed for truth, He found Jesus. It was likely what I call a Divine Appointment. God sent him on a quest for truth and then showed up in a vision to reveal Truth. Before that young man was formed in his mother's womb, God had a plan and a purpose for his life.

In the same way, you and I were carefully designed to fulfill a purpose on this earth. The timing and location of your birth are not accidents. Neither is the family into which you were born.

There is a plan for your life. A purpose for which you have been uniquely created and prepared. And when you discover what it is, expect opposition. It may appear to come from past baggage, your own self-image, or from negative people around you. Regardless whence it comes, its author is the devil.

Opposition is not something a believer needs to fear. The one who is in you is greater than the one that is in the world. Seek Christ. Trust Him. Follow Him. Regardless of what you may believe about Him, He believes in you. He has a plan that sets you apart from others; and He's just waiting to share it with you.

And from each human being, too, I will demand an accounting for the life of another human being. (Genesis 9:4-5).

The death of any innocent human being is a direct assault on the image of the Living God. That is one reason that I volunteer as a peer counselor with an organization that provides truth, hope, and practical help for young women who find themselves pregnant in the midst of very difficult circumstances. I don't want to see any woman duped by the lies of the deliberately ignorant into believing that she is only removing an inconvenient blob of tissue.

By the time a woman knows that she is pregnant, the embryo already has a beating heart, a rapidly-growing brain, and a God-ordained life-plan. Every aspect of a human being from his sex to race, eye color, height, athleticism, intelligence, etc. is encoded into the embryo at the time of conception. Every chromosome in the egg and sperm has been meticulously designed; and unless an interruption occurs the child will continue to grow and develop according to God's unique design plan.

Just because a child displays a characteristic that man calls a defect doesn't mean that he or she should be killed. Even those who display characteristics that are considered terminal conditions are God's workmanship. A woman who would not dream of ripping limb from limb a two-year-old who was diagnosed with untreatable cancer will often condemn a pre-born terminally ill child to just such a death. A mother's womb should be the safest place on earth; sadly these days it's become a place of unspeakable horror.

The basic differences between an embryo and a newborn are the same as between a newborn and a 25-year-old – age and development.

There is no gray area in the choice/life debate. Abortion is murder for hire. My beliefs on this subject are carved in stone: *You shall not commit murder. (Exodus 20:13).* To violate this command is to launch a direct assault on the very image of God. *Whoever sheds human blood, by humans shall their blood be shed; for in the image of God has God made mankind. (Genesis 9:6).*

Please do not misunderstand. I am not advocating violence against abortionists. The solution for them is prayer, evangelism, and legislation. God is sovereign and He reserves life and death decisions to Himself. He takes murder personally. Those who persist in this practice will face His wrath.

But God is also good and merciful, providing hope for all sinners, even those who've committed murder (abortion or not). In His infinite mercy God allowed His one and only Son to be executed to pay for each of our sins, no matter what they may be.

Our God waits with outstretched arms to bring forgiveness, healing, peace, and joy to anyone who will repent and genuinely seek Him. All of your sins and mine were still in the future when Christ died for us. He knows your whole story, yet He delights in you and He is big enough to handle whatever you bring to Him...

For God so loved the world that He gave His one and only Son, that whoever believes in Him shall not perish but have eternal life. For God did not send His Son into the world to condemn the world, but to save the world through Him. Whoever believes in Him is not condemned, but whoever does not believe stands condemned already because they have not believed in the name of God's one and only Son.

This is the verdict: Light has come into the world, but people loved darkness instead of light because their deeds were evil. Everyone who does evil hates the light, and will not come into the light for fear that their deeds will be exposed. But whoever lives by the truth comes into the light, so that it may be seen plainly that what they have done has been done in the sight of God. (John 3:16-21)

Be strong and very courageous. Be careful to obey all the law my servant Moses gave you; do not turn from it to the right or to the left, that you may be successful wherever you go. Keep this Book of the law always on your lips; meditate on it day and night, so that you may be careful to do everything written in it. They you will be prosperous and successful. Have I not commanded you? Be strong and courageous. Do not be afraid; do not be discouraged, for the LORD your God will be with you wherever you go. (Joshua 1:7-9)

As the Israelites approached the Jordan River, again, they had spent 40 years wandering in the wilderness, one year for each day the 12 spies had spent observing and partaking of the abundance God had prepared for them. The generation of adults who had packed up kith and kin to follow Moses out of slavery in Egypt, the ones who saw the wonders and miracles God had done in Egypt for their deliverance, the ones who had walked through the Red Sea on dry ground and watched their Egyptian pursuers washed away in that sea - horses, chariots and all, that entire generation was now dead. Only three men had survived: Moses, Caleb, and Joshua. The rest had been either teenagers or children at the time of the rebellion, or they had been born in the wilderness.

Now Moses was dead, too. And Joshua was charged with guiding this new generation, who had literally grown up in the wilderness, into the land their fathers had lacked the courage and faith to possess. Little wonder God instructed Joshua five times in the first two paragraphs of the book of Joshua to have courage and not be afraid. God had shown so much grace to the Israelites in the face of rampant disobedience and rebellion after they left Egypt, relenting from destroying them each time Moses had prayed for their forgiveness.

This new generation had seen the devastating outcome of their fathers' stiff-necked disobedience. They had wandered through the wilderness, driving their herds and burying their parents along the way, until at last only Joshua and Caleb remained from that faithless generation. I wonder whether they harbored bitterness over all the battles they fought in the wilderness, and the years of abundance they missed out on while they wandered down those pointless roads to nowhere. Set up camp, pack up camp, walk from here to there. Set up camp. Pack up Camp. Walk from here to there...

It must have been a very hard life. Disobedience invariably brings hardship for the spouse and children of those who choose rebellion over God's plan and purpose for him or her. Parents too often sacrifice their children's future on the altar of selfishness or pride.

The new generation of Israelites had learned from their fathers' sinful mistakes, and when it was their time to decide whether they would follow God or lead their own children astray, they chose God. And they enjoyed the financial and material bounty their fathers had been afraid to claim. Moreover they experienced the miraculous as they watched God fight their battles for them, driving out the very tribes and nations their fathers had feared with such ruinous results. Even if your parents led you into the wilderness, it's still your choice whether you stay there or follow God out.

Without God's grace they too would have died in the wilderness. Instead they enjoyed blessing throughout their generation. When it was time to cross the Jordan River into Canaan, the river was at flood stage, but the people were led safely across by the Word of God.

The tablets on which the Law had been written were carried by the Priests inside the Ark of the Covenant. The Israelites crossed the Jordan River on dry ground, but their leaders, the Priests, had to get their feet wet. The waters didn't part until they took those first steps of faith into the rushing waters of the river.

The contrast between generations makes you stop and ask: Where are you leading your family? Today God's complete word is right there, readily available in print or on the Internet. Are you willing to get your feet wet, accept God's offer of grace, and step out in faith to follow God?

Consecrate yourselves for tomorrow the Lord will do amazing things among you. (Joshua 3:5)

The Heavens declare the glory of God; the skies proclaim the work of His hands. Day after day they pour forth speech; night after night they reveal knowledge. They have no speech, they use no words; no sound is heard from them. Yet their voice goes out into all the earth, their words to the ends of the world. (Psalm 19:1-4)

The year was 1968, a year filled with turmoil that eclipses even the cultural shambles in which we find ourselves today. The year began with the USS Pueblo being seized by North Korea and its officers and crew starved and tortured. The next few months were some of the bloodiest of the Vietnam War with daily body counts broadcast on the evening news becoming as commonplace as the day's baseball scores.

As Spring swelled into Summer violence boiled over into the streets at home as racial tensions and the anti-whatever movements took to the streets. The Democratic National Convention was besieged by violent protests in the streets. Both Martin Luther King, Jr. and Robert Kennedy were murdered and their tragic deaths replayed again and again on the evening news.

As summer heat melted into fall the nation breathed a corporate sigh of relief as Apollo 7 launched and returned safely to earth. It had been less than two years since we had lost the Apollo 1 crew, Command Pilot Virgil I. "Gus" Grissom, Senior Pilot Edward H. White II, and Pilot Roger P Chaffee. They had perished in a fire in the Command Module during a launch pad test just weeks before their scheduled launch date. In the early days of the space program, astronauts were as well-known as sports and entertainment stars. Their deaths left a huge scar on the collective hearts of a nation. The success the Apollo 7 Mission restored our sense of hope.

Meanwhile, the presidential campaign heated up as candidates Richard Nixon, Hubert Humphrey, and George Wallace (and we thought the lack of good choices was something new) duked it out for the White House. Nixon was narrowly elected; but the Democratic Party maintained their grip on the legislature. Even my teenage excitement over going on my first "real" date couldn't dispel the sense of impending doom that seemed to fill the air.

The Christmas Season arrived in the usual manner in my hometown of Savannah, ushered in the day after Thanksgiving with our annual Christmas Parade. Santa, as always, brought up the rear of the parade, and proceeded directly to the Toy Department at the Sears Roebuck store on Henry Street. Things brightened a bit as lights went up, trees were decorated, and brightly wrapped gifts appeared beneath.

But still there was this constant sense of some unknown impending doom. Among all the intense highs and lows of the year, the most exciting was yet to come.

On December 21, Apollo 8 was launched in the heavens, and for the first time, man prepared to orbit the moon. There was another huge national sigh of relief two days later when the crew of the USS Pueblo was finally released, and the battered and weary men began the journey home.

But the thing I remember most about that year was the Christmas Eve broadcast by the crew of the Apollo 8. We saw the "dark side of the moon" for the first time and got our first look at ourselves from another place in the universe. It was surreal, overwhelming, and humbling all at the same time. It forever altered my view of creation as I began to comprehend its vastness, and of myself as I began to comprehend my smallness. Then came the message.

To understand the significance of the message it is important to understand the men who chose its content. Commander Frank Borman was a career Air Force officer. He had served as a fighter pilot, an operational pilot and instructor, an experimental test pilot and an assistant professor of Thermodynamics and Fluid Mechanics at West Point. When selected by NASA, he was serving as an instructor at the Aerospace Research Pilot School at Edwards AFB, California.

Lunar Module Pilot, Bill Anders had received a Bachelor of Science degree from the United States Naval Academy and a Master of Science degree in Nuclear Engineering from the Air Force Institute of Technology at Wright-Patterson Air Force Base. Anders was commissioned in the Air Force after graduation from the Naval Academy and served as a fighter pilot in all-weather interception squadrons of the Air Defense Command and later was responsible for technical management of nuclear power reactor shielding and radiation effects programs while at the Air Force Weapons Laboratory in New Mexico. In 1964, Anders was selected by NASA as an astronaut with responsibilities for dosimetry, radiation effects and environmental controls.

Command Module Pilot and Navigator, Jim Lovell, had received a Bachelor of Science degree from the United States Naval Academy. During his Naval career he had numerous aviator assignments, including a 4-year tour as a test pilot at the Naval Air Test Center, Patuxent River, Maryland. While there he served as Program Manager for the F4H "Phantom" Fighter. A graduate of the Aviation Safety School of the University of Southern

California, he also served as Safety Engineer with the Fighter Squadron 101 at the Naval Air Station, Oceana, Virginia.

All three of the Apollo 8 crew members were highly intelligent men of science which makes their message all the more powerful. Given free rein by their superiors at NASA to compose the script for the historic broadcast, it began,

In the beginning God created the heaven and the earth. And the earth was without form and void; and darkness was upon the face of the deep. And the Spirit of God moved upon the face of the waters.

And God said, Let there be light: And there was light. And God saw the light, that it was good: and God divided the light from the darkness. And God called the light Day; and the darkness He called Night.

And the evening and the morning were the first day.

And God said, Let there be a firmament in the midst of the waters, and let it divide the waters from the waters. And God made the firmament, and divided the waters that were under the firmament from the waters that were above the firmament: and it was so.

And God called the firmament Heaven. And the evening and the morning were the second day.

And God said, Let the waters under the heaven be gathered together into one place and let the dry land appear: and it was so.

And God called the dry land Earth and the gathering together of the waters called He seas: and God saw that it was good. (Genesis 1:1-10)

I can imagine no more perfect text than the one that they chose to read from the first chapter of Genesis. Thanks to YouTube, their broadcast is available to a new generation as well as to those of us who simply enjoy reliving those breathtaking moments in History.

Elections and politicians come and go. The church is often as guilty as the world of putting too much confidence in what man can and cannot do. So, whatever your politics, find peace and joy in the realization that nothing has truly changed since God first spoke those four little words that sent shock waves through eternity: Let there be light. There's still room for hope. He hasn't changed. He's still God. He watches from His throne of judgment as the unbelieving of this world parade past into eternal damnation.

God is still in control. And He still loves you. Just as, for one miraculous moment in time, the astronauts of Apollo 8 refocused the world's attention, let's keep our focus on the Creator of Heaven and Earth.

I am the Lord your God, who brought you out of Egypt, out of the land of slavery. You shall have no other gods before me. (Exodus 20:2-3)

It is so easy in the busy-ness of life to become distracted by the madness and confusion around us; and sometimes it is the pretty things -- the shiny baubles of success and wealth that distract us most. The former often lead to fear and discouragement, the latter to greed and pride. Either way, when we allow them to turn our eyes from the LORD our God, we make them into our personal little gods. Whatever consumes the majority of our resources, our thoughts and our time, whatever we value most, that is our god.

We work hard in order to provide for the basic needs of our families. But if the job, the business opportunity, the money, the things the money buys, or our families become the momentum that propels us through our day, we can easily lose sight of our Creator, and the purpose for which He placed us in the job, gave us the opportunity, arranged the location of the home, provided the financial resources, and prioritizes the spiritual well-being of our family members.

We sometimes function like a point-and-shoot camera, focusing on whatever happens to be front and center in our field of vision. We become consumed by what is seen. But God's Word says, *fix (your) eyes not on what is seen, but on what is unseen. For what is seen is temporary, but what is unseen is eternal... Let us fix our eyes on Jesus, the author and perfecter of our faith, Who for the joy set before Him endured the cross, scorning its shame, and sat down at the right hand of the throne of God." (2 Corinthians 4:18; Hebrews 12:2)*

God is the original Creator and Entrepreneur. He knows the hearts and minds of, as well as His plans and purposes for, every person on earth. He is the ultimate networker, able to arrange divine appointments to fulfill His purposes for us. He cares more about your family than you do. He can arrange your day and order your life to provide success that you cannot imagine. And He can do it without leaving a trail of wasted time, mistakes, missed opportunities, or regrets. But you must be focused on Him in order to follow where He is leading.

His common purpose for each of us is to honor Him with our lives, and to expand His kingdom so that none will spend eternity apart from Him. His top priority for those with whom He brings us into contact is their spiritual well-being, whether in family, social, or business relationships. But always our relationship with Him is fundamental to the success of everything else in our lives. Live each day in anticipation of His return.

How does His life/business plan for us look?

"...let us be self-controlled, putting on faith and love as a breastplate, and the hope of salvation as a helmet. For God did not appoint us to suffer wrath but to receive salvation through our Lord Jesus Christ. He died for us so that, whether we are awake or asleep, we may live together with Him. Therefore encourage one another and build each other up, just as in fact you are doing.

Now we ask you, brothers, to respect those who work hard among you, who are over you in the Lord and who admonish you. Hold them in the highest regard in love because of their work. Live in peace with each other. And we urge you, brothers, warn those who are idle, encourage the timid, help the weak, be patient with everyone. Make sure that nobody pays back wrong for wrong, but always try to be kind to each other and to everyone else.

Be joyful always; pray continually, give thanks in all circumstances, for this is God's will for you in Christ Jesus. Do not put out the Spirit's fire; do not treat prophecies with contempt. Test everything. Hold on to the good. Avoid every kind of evil.

May God Himself, the God of peace, sanctify you through and through. May your whole spirit, soul and body be kept blameless at the coming of our Lord Jesus Christ. The one who calls you is faithful and He will do it. (1 Thessalonians 5:8-24)

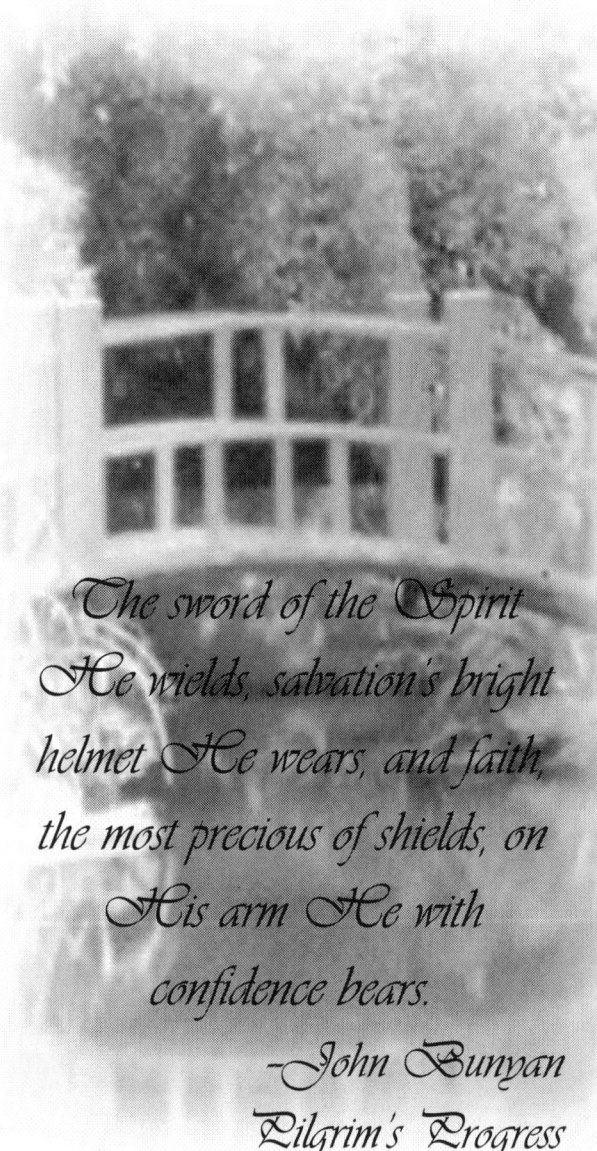

The sword of the Spirit
He wields, salvation's bright
helmet He wears, and faith,
the most precious of shields, on
His arm He with
confidence bears.
—John Bunyan
Pilgrim's Progress

Part Five

Then in fellowship sweet
We will sit at His feet,
Or we'll walk by His side in the way;
What He says we will do;
Where He sends, we will go,
Never fear, only trust and obey.

Jesus replied, 'I tell you the truth, everyone who sins is a slave to sin. Now a slave has no permanent place in the family, but a son belongs to it forever. So if the Son sets you free, you will be free indeed. (John 8:34-36)

was counselling a while back with a young woman who has had a lot of difficulty in her life, partly because of her own failures, partly from the failures of those around her. Although as a child she had learned of the love of Christ from her grandmother, she has spent a number of years in the wilderness, pushed and pulled by temptations, her feelings, and life in general. Avoiding God because of a sense of guilt and shame, she experienced a long season of loss and failure.

I had often assured her of God's unchanging love; encouraging her to spend time with Him in prayer and Bible study. I urged her to find a church family where she could be involved in serving Him and cultivating friendships with people who can help her to grow in her faith.

She called a few days ago to share her excitement after attending church for the first time in quite a while. All her apprehensions had melted away as she was welcomed by the people there, and began to worship God in fellowship with other believers.

She expressed relief that she is forgiven now and if she dies she will not have to go to hell. While wandering in the wilderness she had forgotten about God's grace. She had come to believe that she had somehow lost her salvation in one of the many pits she had stumbled, fallen, or jumped into during her days in the wilderness.

I don't know what her relationship with God really is. I was not there when as a child she made the decision to trust Him. But I believe it was sincere and I know that the enemy has thrown everything under the sun at her to destroy the seed of faith that was planted in her heart. Despite everything, she always returns to the desire to be close to God.

More important than anything I know about her, I know the God who saves. Therefore, I believe that she is a child of God. Not because of anything she has done; she did not save herself. Not because of the strength of her faith; she has faltered many times. Not because there was always a longing to return to Him, although there was. I believe because of Grace.

The Bible teaches that you cannot lose your salvation because you cannot earn it. It is a gift, freely given through the grace of God. Although you may set the gift on a shelf for a while, thus showing contempt for the giver, He doesn't withdraw the gift. Jesus made that clear in the story of the Prodigal Son. (See Luke 15:11-32).

When the prodigal finally "came to his senses" and humbly returned to his father's house, he was warmly, and with great celebration, welcomed home - a beloved son. He had missed many wonderful days with his father and suffered much hardship and loss while he was in the wilderness. But because he returned in genuine repentance, all was forgiven and restoration was complete. And his father dealt with the brother who resented the Prodigal's return.

His brother had chosen the better path, never feeling the gnawing hunger of guilt and regret. He had seen the grace his father showed to servants, friends, and family. His fellowship with his father was intact, but for a brief moment the brother forgot that what really mattered was the relationship.

Salvation is based solely upon Christ's redeeming work on our behalf, and He is trustworthy. He spent His incarnate life faithfully resisting every temptation known to man so that you and I could be covered with His righteousness. When I face the final judgment and God asks why He should let me into His heaven I won't have to say a word. Jesus will lovingly take me by the hand and welcome me Home. I belong to Him because He set me free.

Therefore, brothers and sisters, since we have confidence to enter the Most Holy Place by the blood of Jesus, ...that is, his body, and since we have a great priest over the house of God, let us draw near to God with a sincere heart and with the full assurance that faith brings, having our hearts sprinkled to cleanse us from a guilty conscience and having our bodies washed with pure water. Let us hold unswervingly to the hope we profess, for he who promised is faithful. And let us consider how we may spur one another on toward love and good deeds, not giving up meeting together, as some are in the habit of doing, but encouraging one another. (Hebrews 10:19-25)

I once heard a preacher tell the story of a farmer named John, who had stopped attending church services. On his way home one wintry evening John's pastor decided to stop by the farm for a visit. John was startled and a bit nervous when he opened the door to find his pastor standing there, but invited him in and offered him a seat beside the fire.

They sat quietly for a few moments, John dreading the rebuke he was certain would come. But the pastor said nothing. He silently picked up the fireplace tongs and, taking a glowing coal from the middle of the fire, he laid it by itself on the hearth. Quietly they watched the blaze die and the once-brilliant ember become dark, cold, and hard. John got the point and assured the departing pastor that he would see him Sunday morning at worship.

But that response isn't typical of what we often see happening today. Today's prodigals say church is full of hypocrites, or that it is not relevant to their lives, or they can worship as easily in a deer stand or on the beach beholding the wonders of God's creation as they can in church.

All of these justifications may reflect personal experiences, but that may be more the result of an improper attitude on the part of the prodigal than a flaw of the church in general.

The church always has and always will have her problems, but that's simply because she's made up of imperfect people who will behave inconsistently at times. If we could live a sinless life, we would have no need of a Savior. We must not commit the sin of rejecting the Savior because of the sins of others.

Worship the LORD with gladness; come before Him with joyful songs. Know that the LORD is God. It is He who made us, and we are His. (Psalm 100:2-3)

God created us for relationship with Him. God is intolerant of deliberate or cherished sin in our lives because of the damage it does to us and to those around us. Sin creates distance between God and us. It destroys the intimacy of our relationships with Him. He disciplines His children for our own good. He loves us more than life as He demonstrated on the cross; and when we stray from His presence, He comes after us as the Good Shepherd He portrays in His Word.

Then Jesus told them this parable: *'Suppose one of you has a hundred sheep and loses one of them. Does he not leave the ninety-nine in the open country and go after the lost sheep until he finds it? And when he finds it, he joyfully puts it on his shoulders and goes home. Then he calls his friends and neighbors together and says, Rejoice with me; I have found my lost sheep. I tell you that in the same way there will be more rejoicing in heaven over one sinner who repents than over ninety-nine righteous persons who do not need to repent. (Luke 15:3-7)*

I have strayed many times in my life but I know that although I was sometimes out of God's presence, I was never out of His sight. When He came after me, it was as the father of the prodigal child. He watched me for evidence that I was ready to give up the sin to which I'd clung so tightly. I've never had to clean myself up or find my way back home. He has always gently lifted me out of whatever pit I was in and lovingly restored the intimacy that I had destroyed.

With God, condemnation never follows repentance, only the peace and joy that come from being forgiven and restored. God's Discipline is about teaching, not punishment. His purpose is that we will learn to serve Him faithfully.

God, our perfect Father, knows that allowing us to suffer the consequences of our behavior is the best way for us to learn the error of our way. When we refuse to learn, He will permit, or even cause events that shock us into reality. Rehab centers, hospitals, and prisons are heavily populated with people who have strayed from their relationships with Christ into the downward spiral of sin. Those blue lights in the rear-view mirror just may have been sent by God to prevent the speeding ticket or fatal accident that awaits just up the road, because someone was driving under the influence of drugs or alcohol, or possibly just going too fast.

Thus, when I have strayed from God I did not lose my value to Him, only my usefulness to Him. Those times in the wilderness were wasted times

-- whether hours, days, years, or even decades. When I returned, the fellowship was always just as sweet; but, oh, what I had missed.

God has a timeline for my life upon which He's laid out opportunities to serve Him as well as spiritual, physical, relationship, and material blessings. Many of those gifts were either left unopened or given to those who remained faithful to their relationship to Him, while I wandered foolishly in the wilderness living on the swill of rebellion – more useful to the devil than to my Savior. Make no mistake, when you are not serving God you are serving Satan.

As Joshua said to the Israelites after they had come out of the wilderness, crossed the Jordan River, and finally taken possession of the Promised Land:

Now fear the Lord and serve Him with all faithfulness. Throw away the gods your forefathers worshiped beyond the River and in Egypt, and serve the Lord. But if serving the Lord seems undesirable to you, then choose for yourselves this day whom you will serve ... But as for me and my household, we will serve the Lord. (Joshua 24:14-15)

Only let us live up to what we have already attained. (Philippians 3:16)

 watch with amusement and a bit of incredulity the madness that has come to be called Black Friday. It's the day when retail sales in this country typically move from red (loss) to black (profit), hence the name. For many shoppers, it is the day when "Christmas Shopping Season" officially begins. Traditionally, it falls on the Friday following Thanksgiving Day; but sadly has spilled over to begin the afternoon of Thanksgiving Day.

Serious "Black Friday" shoppers have spent the week studying newspaper and Internet ads, looking for the best price on just the right gift for each person on their list. With hawkish resolve they plan their assault. Most retailers have "specials" at designated hours when a few items are heavily discounted, the bait on the hook that pulls the shoppers into their store (where presumably they will also buy non-discounted items). The hawks swoop in and grab the "special" and move on to the next location.

Sometimes the chaos that follows the opening of the doors resembles the frenzy of feeding time at Gatorland. People have been seriously injured, and one big box store employee was trampled to death a couple of years ago. All to save a few dollars on "stuff".

I do strive to shop as wisely as I can; but there is nothing for sale in any store anywhere in the world that I want badly enough to fight for it. Since I don't enjoy shopping, I'm not taking a moral high road here; I simply don't get the attraction.

But, wouldn't it be wonderful if we could get the world that excited about our Savior. What are we, the purveyors of the Gospel, doing wrong? I think the answer is marketing. Our advertising is ineffective at best, offensive at worst. Our customer service is often deficient or nonexistent.

What attributes mark the daily lives of believers that reveal the value and beauty of our Savior? It is becoming increasingly common to encounter people who have never darkened the doorway of a church building or picked up a Bible.

As followers of Christ, we possess the most precious and desirable treasure in all creation: Salvation, by the Grace of God, through Faith in Jesus Christ. Just because salvation is free to us, doesn't mean that we should treat it as something cheap. The price that Christ paid on the cross is the dearest ever paid.

But, what of His character can be seen in our daily lives? Do we accurately represent Him in our little corner of the world? If we lived in a place where following Christ is a crime, would there be enough evidence to convict us? Would anyone look at us and call us a friend of God as Abraham was called?

We are living in Babylon just as surely as Abraham did. We pursue material wealth, lust after vampires, indulge addictions, and worship sex. Our culture is becoming as debauched and hedonistic as any pagan society in the annals of history; meanwhile the church tiptoes through the minefield of tolerance and political correctness as if we are ashamed of the Gospel of Jesus Christ.

Yes, the lost around us have the God-given freedom to choose to go to hell. But should we not make certain that the choice they make is fully informed? They do not see what is wrong with them because they see their own reflection when they look at us, rather than the reflection of the One who saved us and now indwells us.

As long as the world sees the same people stumbling out of the clubs on Saturday night as they see walking into church on Sunday morning, or hear the co-worker with the framed Bible verse on his office wall using profanity in the break room, or watch the man and woman who sing in the choir engage in an adulterous relationship, or the Deacon businessman using unethical tactics to get ahead, or Christian wives abandoning husband and marriage because they are unhappy, etc. As long as so-called Christians live in a way that belies the regenerate nature of Salvation, the world will continue to spiral downward into depravity.

Being a friend of God does not mean being perfect. Abraham was far from perfect; he made many mistakes. But Abraham followed the path that God laid out for him. He worshipped only the one true God. The people he encountered knew there was something different about him. And they knew that the difference was in Abraham's relationship to the living God.

I want to know Christ--yes, to know the power of his resurrection and participation in his sufferings, becoming like him in his death, and so, somehow, attaining to the resurrection from the dead.

Not that I have already obtained all this, or have already arrived at my goal, but I press on to take hold of that for which Christ Jesus took hold of me. Brothers and sisters, I do not consider myself yet to have taken hold of it. But one thing I do: Forgetting what is behind and straining toward what is ahead, I press on toward the goal to win the prize for which God has called me heavenward in Christ Jesus. All of us, then, who are mature should take such a view of things. And if on some point you think differently, that too God will make clear to you. Only let us live up to what we have already attained. (Philippians 3:8-16)

After they had mocked Him, they took off the robe and put His own clothes on Him. Then they led Him away to crucify Him. (Matthew 27:31)

Meekness seems to have lost its place of honor in this age of superheroes and power lunches. Although it's possible that we simply no longer understand what it means. Modern dictionaries define it as: weak, easily imposed upon, docile. We equate meekness with weakness, but there is a vast difference between the two.

The Greek root from which meek was translated is *praus*, which is a term that is used in horse training. It's the process by which a wild horse is brought into submission to its rider; and in Jesus' day was used to describe the training of a war horse.

Only the bravest and most powerful horses were trained for battle. They had to possess the same character traits as their riders: courage, strength, loyalty, and the will to stand and fight when everything in them said to run away and save themselves. A weak-willed horse could be trained to pull a wagon, but only the most audacious would stand in battle.

Our Savior is easily the most audacious man who ever lived. As God, He created everything out of nothing. He has legions of angels at His command. He walked on water, healed the sick, raised the dead, turned water into the fruit of the unbruised grape, calmed storms, cast out demons, resisted every temptation known to man, and then laid down His life for my salvation.

One of my favorite stories from the Bible tells of the day when Jesus drove the money-changers out of the Temple. He didn't run willy-nilly into the Temple court screaming and randomly overturning tables. The Gospel of John says, *And making a whip of cords, He drove them all out of the temple, with sheep and oxen. And He poured out the coins of the money-changers and overturned their tables. (John 2:15).*

Taking the time to sit patiently braiding cords into a whip is definitely not the action of someone who is out of control. Life is often unnerving, but always an adventure for those who attempt to truly follow Christ. I can just imagine the Twelve whispering among themselves, "What do you think He's going to do with that whip?"

It is not weakness, but the meekness of Christ that is clearly revealed at His crucifixion. He voluntarily set aside the mantle of absolute power in order to lay down His life.

He fulfilled His Father's purpose for Him – just as He had when He entered history as an infant - at the mercy of His creation, but in the heart of His Father's will.

Jesus is the ultimate war horse – infinite, fearless power under the command of Jehovah God. In His birth, He traversed the chasm that sin had created between God and man. In His death, He won the battle over sin on my behalf. In His resurrection He defeated death for all eternity. Through His Holy Spirit He infuses me with His power so that having been "meeked" with the yoke of obedience, I can find rest in the midst of the battles that He calls me to fight.

The meek will not inherit the earth because they are weak, but because they were obedient to stand firm in the battle.

Blessed are the meek, for they shall inherit the earth. (Matthew 5:5)

Shout for joy to the LORD, all the earth. Worship the LORD with gladness; come before Him with joyful songs. Know that the LORD is God. It is He who made us, and we are His; we are His people, the sheep of His pasture. Enter His gates with thanksgiving and His courts with praise; give thanks to Him and praise His name. For the LORD is good and His love endures forever; His faithfulness continues through all generations. (Psalm 100)

Thanksgiving Day is a major holiday in the United States, known largely these days for family, food, and football. Like so many holidays it has lost focus. Many Americans seem to have forgotten that to be thankful for something, you must be thankful to Someone. For every provision there must be a provider. So we have lost our true sense of gratitude and replaced it with a sense of entitlement.

But is that not the typical outcome of misplaced gratitude? We have attributed our sense of security and provision to our own abilities, the government, or the military. The upshot is we have sacrificed gratitude on the altar of pride; or we founder in a sea of insecurity because we live in uncertain times.

This was not always so. Revisionist historians aside, the majority of our founders believed in the providence of God. They were intent on securing for future generations the blessing of freedom to worship God without government interference. They were very mindful that, like Gideon and Joshua in Old Testament days, the battles for our freedom were won as surely by the providence of God as the blood of patriots.

George Washington's 1789 Presidential Proclamation summed up the mindset and belief system of our founding fathers:

"Whereas it is the duty of all nations to acknowledge the providence of Almighty God, to obey His will, to be grateful for His benefits, and humbly implore His protection and favor; and whereas both Houses of Congress have, by their joint committee, requested me to recommend to the people of the United States a day of Public Thanksgiving and Prayer, to be observed by acknowledging with grateful hearts the many signal favors of Almighty God, especially by affording them an opportunity peaceably to establish a form of government for their safety and happiness.

Now therefore I do recommend and assign Thursday the twenty-six of November next, to be devoted by the people of these States to the service of that Great and Glorious Being, who is the Beneficent Author of all the good that was, that is, or that will be; that we may then all unite in rendering unto Him our sincere and humble thanks for His kind care and protection of the people of this country, previous to their becoming a nation; for the single manifold mercies, and the favorable interpositions of His providence, in the courage and conclusion of the late war; for the great degree of tranquility, union and plenty which we have since enjoyed; for the peaceable and rational manner in which we have been enabled to establish Constitutions of Government for our safety and happiness, and particularly the national one now instituted; for the civil and religious liberty with which we are blessed, and the means we have of acquiring and diffusing useful knowledge; and in general, for all the great and various favors which He has been pleased to confer upon us.

And also, that we may then unite in most humbly offering our prayers and supplications to the Great Lord and Ruler of Nations, and beseech Him to pardon our national and other transgressions; to enable us all, whether in public or private institutions, to perform our several and relative duties properly and punctually; to render our National Government a blessing to all the people, by constantly being a government of wise, just, and constitutional laws, discretely and faithfully executed and obeyed; to protect and guide all sovereigns and nations (especially such as have shown kindness to us) and to bless them with good governments, peace and concord; to promote the knowledge and practice of true religion and virtue, and the increase of science, among them and us; and generally, to grant unto all mankind such a degree of temporal prosperity as He alone knows to be best."

As I write this, our country is at war against terrorism. The economy is faltering. Unemployment is high. Families are falling apart. There is adversity and sadness all around. Some days it is hard to have that attitude of gratitude. But, when those days come, I get back to the basics. I am a sinner who deserves to go to hell; but because of the sacrifice of my loving Savior, I will never have to go there.

When I let that truth overtake me, joy consumes me. He is then able to remind me that He is the source for all of my provision. With Him there is security, peace, and joy immeasurable. He is faithful and I am thankful.

For this reason, since the day we heard about you, we have not stopped praying for you and asking God to fill you with the knowledge of His will through all spiritual wisdom and understanding. And we pray this in order that you may live a life worthy of the Lord and may please Him in every way; bearing fruit in every good work, growing in the knowledge of God, being strengthened with all power according to His glorious might so that you may have great endurance and patience and joyfully giving thanks to the Father, Who has qualified you to share in the inheritance of the saints in the kingdom of Light. For He has rescued us from the dominion of darkness and brought us into the kingdom of the Son He loves, in whom we have redemption, the forgiveness of sins. (Colossians 1:9-14)

We sometimes fret over our desire to know God's "will" for our lives; we make life in Christ seem so much more complicated than it actually is. Paul answered the question succinctly in this passage. God's will for all who follow Christ is the same - to live a life worthy of, and pleasing to, Jesus Christ.

That sounds like an impossible dream; and that's what it is when I try to do it without Him. But Jesus never intended for me to do anything without Him. His plan is to live through me. He wants me to know Him and to share my understanding of Him with others both in word and through acts of service. And He equips me through "His glorious might" to serve Him joyfully and with a thankful heart. For me, this service frequently takes the form of words; more often spoken than written.

I've loved words ever since, as a preschooler, I learned to read looking on as my mother helped my older sisters with their reading homework. I think that's one of the reasons I love God's Word so much, the writing is masterful. I love a well-crafted sentence or paragraph. From the lyrical artistry of the Psalms to the magnificent narrative of the Pentateuch to the passionate apologetic of the Gospels of Luke and John and the sometimes unnerving imagery of the Prophecies, it stimulates my imagination and thrills my soul.

God has taught me so much through His Word and, over time, through His Spirit. I have done quite a bit of counseling and spoken encouragement, but to my shame, I spent many years hiding the written lessons from those who might have found comfort or help - those for whom they were actually written. Fear that they would not be accepted kept me from "boldly speaking the truth as I should". Consequently, my life has not always been a true reflection of my faith or my passion for God. I've surely failed to have the full range of influence for which I was created.

I have heard it said that culture is our inward religion turned outward. As I look around at the world in which we live, I think far too many followers of Christ must have been as timid as I have. If our culture accurately displays the collective conscience of our nation, reflecting the deepest beliefs of the majority of the citizenry, then clearly far too many of us have bowed to the religions of pride, political correctness, and tolerance.

The price Jesus paid for us was far too dear to be treated so carelessly. Most of us face no greater risk for our faith than to be rejected or ostracized by others.

Meanwhile, the persecuted church grows in depth and numbers throughout parts of Europe, Africa, and Asia. Believers, who often have limited access to Bibles or training, suffer and die for refusing to deny the name of Jesus Christ. Yet the Western Church, well-equipped, well-educated and free to speak boldly, remains impotent for fear of being thought intolerant.

Jesus trained a handful of mostly under-educated, blue-collar men and women. Facing torture and martyr's deaths, they turned the world upside down by boldly proclaiming the Gospel of the resurrected Christ.

Perhaps if we lived more like the first followers of Christ, the Church wouldn't be intimidated into silence in the most free nation in the world. I wonder what the world would look like if we looked more like Him.

...His sheep follow Him because they know His voice. (John 10:4)

It has been my experience that God speaks to His people in many ways. First, and always trustworthy, is His written Word, the Holy Bible. He miraculously breathed His truth into the hearts and minds of those who sought Him in ancient days; and over time He guided the compilation of a complete-enough record of the story of His interaction with His creation. His Word contains all the information that is necessary for anyone who approaches it with an open heart to find Him.

He has also spoken to me many times through the written or spoken words of other believers. Anything that comes from God will always be in agreement with His written Word. He sometimes uses other people to focus or confirm a message that He has for you or me at a moment in time. But if it the message truly comes from Him, it will always point you to His Word.

Sometimes He speaks to me directly through His Spirit, into my spirit. Recognizing His voice can be a delicate process, but it's one that He is anxious to simplify. He desires an intimate relationship with His followers. He wants us to know His voice.

The last few years of my life have been extreme in the confusion and insanity that has surrounded me. Just within our immediate families there has been betrayal, adultery, murder, substance abuse, prison, and the discord of opposing beliefs about all of it.

It was easy to know what is right and what is wrong in each situation, the written Word has all the answers. But, the day-to-day relationship issues are more complicated. I was bombarded with so many voices that I just needed to hear His voice. In desperation I asked Him to teach me to recognize His voice.

The answer didn't come in the way I expected. What I heard was a very gentle and familiar voice saying, "Wash your hands". My response was, "How odd". Again, "Wash your hands". So I did, many times each day for several weeks.

I am already very conscientious when it comes to hygiene, but this was extreme. I asked several times, "Is this you, Lord?" The reply was always "Yes".

The point of course was never that I should follow odd and irrelevant rituals, but that I would know His voice. That voice is as familiar to me now as my own husband's voice. Why would He tell me to wash my hands? Simple answer. I keep an index card stuck in the corner of my vanity mirror with whatever scripture I am currently meditating on or memorizing written on it.

The Holy Spirit was bringing me back full-circle to His Word, the starting point of most encounters with Christ. It's so much easier to follow Christ consistently, if you spend time each day reading, studying, and meditating on His Word.

God's Word has sustained me in the hard times, radically altered my view of this world, renewed my mind, and changed my heart. His Word always draws us nearer to Him. He's no respecter of persons. That's why He still chooses the foolish things of this world to confound the wise, and speaks to the most ordinary of His sheep. Like me, each time I sit down to write.

Come let us bow down in worship, let us kneel before the Lord our Maker; for He is our God and we are the people of His pasture, the flock under His care. Today if you hear His voice, do not harden your hearts... (Psalm 95:6-8)

And when you pray, do not be like the hypocrites, for they love to pray standing in the synagogues and on the street corners to be seen by men. I tell you the truth, they have received their reward in full. But when you pray, go into your room, close the door and pray to your Father, who is unseen. Then your Father, who sees what is done in secret, will reward you. And when you pray, do not keep on babbling like pagans, for they think they will be heard because of their many words. Do not be like them, for your Father knows what you need before you ask Him. (Matthew 6:5-8)

Every New Year finds me pondering resolutions, although I seldom make them (never had much success keeping them). But this year I have become intrigued by those made nearly three centuries ago by a young man on the cusp of beginning his ministry.

Born in 1703 to Reverend Timothy Edwards, a Congregational minister and his wife, Esther Stoddard Edwards, Jonathan Edwards has been described as "The first and greatest homegrown American philosopher". Yale educated, he studied the Bible along with the arts, science, and great philosophers. His academic credentials were impeccable, his passion for God undeniable.

He pastored the Northampton Congregational Church in Massachusetts for more than two decades before moving into frontier areas of New England to serve as missionary to the Mohawk and Mohican tribes. In 1758, at the age of 55, he became president of The College of New Jersey, now Princeton University. He died a short time later from a reaction to an immunization he had received; but what a life he had lived.

A prolific writer and pragmatic preacher, he is credited with stimulating the birth of the First Great Awakening in the 1730's. His most famous sermon is certainly *Sinners in the Hands of an Angry God*, which when delivered in 1741 to an apathetic church, brought repentance, revival, and many conversions.

It was while he was in graduate school at Yale that he made his resolutions. As a young man, about to embark on a journey of service to God, he took time to reflect on the kind of man he wanted to be. He then set about coming up with steps that he could take to shape his character into that man. These steps he resolved that he would do. These were not mere rules by which to live, but a creed by which his character would be developed for the fulfillment of God's purpose for him.

His first resolution states his determination, first and foremost, to glorify God and benefit mankind, establishing the standard by which every decision must be measured: What will this pursuit of mine say about God?

Edwards wrote his resolutions over the course of about eight months and reread them every week for the rest of his life, which undoubtedly explains his success in keeping them.

From childhood on Jonathan Edwards' life was directed by prayer, often combined with fasting. He was known to spend days on end cloistered in his office in prayer. His times of prayer were marked with humility and fervency that were fundamentals of his faithfulness to Christ, and his success as a man, husband, father, preacher, educator, and evangelist.

Resolution 29 reads: *Resolved, never to count that a prayer, nor to let that pass as a prayer, nor that as a petition of a prayer, which is so made, that I cannot hope that God will answer it; nor that as a confession, which I cannot hope God will accept.* It reveals his commitment to making his prayer life both pleasing and acceptable to God. By keeping his focus on the sovereignty of God, Edwards kept himself humble before God, his heart in right relationship to God, and his soul passionate for God.

Of the Edwards' 1394 known descendants there were 13 college presidents, 100 attorneys, 30 judges, 80 public officials in various other positions, 76 military officers, 60 physicians, 60 prominent authors, 100 preachers and missionaries, three United States senators, one Vice President of the United States, and 295 college graduates, among whom were governors of states and ministers to foreign countries.

We live in an age when people behave as if character does not matter, faith is for the simple-minded, and prayer is an exercise in futility. We would do well to examine our hearts, as Edwards did, and prioritize our lives with the sovereignty of God in mind. The impact could change not only our own lives, but likely generations to come.

The effective, fervent prayer of a righteous man avails much. (James 5:16)

Therefore I urge you, brothers and sisters, in view of God's mercy, to offer your bodies as a living sacrifice, holy and pleasing to God – this is your true and proper worship. Do not conform to the pattern of this world, but be transformed by the renewing of your mind. Then you will be able to test and approve what God's will is – His good, pleasing and perfect will. (Romans 12:1-2)

Both now and eternally, believers are called first and foremost to love God with all our hearts, mind, and strength. And we are called to live out that love through obedience to Him. The mysterious thing about a life of obedience to Christ is that it is not burdensome, but leads to both righteousness and joy. The world doesn't know that following Christ brings joy unless they see it in our lives.

Those who claim to be Christians seem to commit adultery, cheat on their taxes, and use profanity at pretty much the same rate as the rest of the world. Some people think that by glossing over the devastating effects of sin and watering down the truth, they make the Gospel more appealing and will reach more people. But in providing the unrepentant or unregenerate with a false sense of spiritual security, they only lead those people farther astray than they were already.

Jesus is the only way to the Father, but He will not work in a heart that's too hard or too proud. Whether you seek salvation or fellowship with God through prayer, Jesus is the only way. I know that is not a popular belief these days, but Jesus said, *I am the way, the truth, and the life. No one comes to the Father except through me. (John 14:6)*.

As the sacrificial lamb, Jesus secured for us an eternity in God's presence. As our High Priest, He serves as intermediary, making intimacy with God possible through prayer, as His spirit intercedes with God the Father, on our behalf.

The cross of Christ is a cross of obedience. Sometimes it brings trials and suffering; but always it brings us close to Him. His love is perfect, unchanging, untarnished. He has purposed to love through us, to work through us, to reach the world through us. As Adrian Rogers used to say, "Holiness is not the way to Christ; Christ is the way to holiness".

I have been crucified with Christ and I no longer live, but Christ lives in me. The life I now live in the body, I live by faith in the Son of God, who loved me and gave himself for me. (Galatians 2:20)

Create in me a pure heart, O God. And renew a steadfast spirit within me. Do not cast me from your presence or take your Holy Spirit from me. Restore to me the joy of your salvation and grant me a willing spirit, to sustain me. (Psalm 51:11)

*S*uppose He did, though. Suppose God decided to withdraw His Holy Spirit from the face of the earth. I wonder how many churches would go on as if nothing had happened. Would they still meet for worship? Would they even notice that He was gone?

I've heard it said that the church isn't an organization with Christ as CEO; it's a living organism with Christ as the head. If His Spirit were gone, would His presence even be missed in many of our churches?

Now the Lord is the Spirit, and where the Spirit of the Lord is, there is freedom. We all, with unveiled faces, are looking as in a mirror at the glory of the Lord and are being transformed into the same image from glory to glory; this is from the Lord who is the Spirit. (2 Corinthians 3:17-18)

What about the individual members of the body? Are we exercising enough of His power in our lives for there to be a conspicuous difference if He were gone? Would our families, our work ethic, our entertainment choices change? Would the divorce rate in the church change?

And do not grieve the Holy Spirit of God, with whom you were sealed for the day of redemption. (Ephesians 4:30). The original Greek word for grieve is *lupeo*, which means to offend or make sorrowful. Rebellion against the leadership of His Holy Spirit is an offensive act, a tearing at the unbreakable fiber of His seal of salvation. Since God exists outside time and space, and Christ died for us before the foundation of the world, the continued sin of a believer is especially scornful to the One who paid such an agonizing price to secure his salvation. Sin damages fellowship between the believer and our heavenly Father.

Still God placed His Spirit within His children as a mark of His ownership. His is the voice that calls us to repentance and freedom from the weight of sin. His power swells up within the soul, according the strength and resolve to live in freedom from the guilt of the past. His faithfulness nurtures hope for the future, and confidence in His unchanging love.

Do not quench the Spirit. (1 Thessalonians 5:19). The original Greek word for quench is *sbennumi*, which means to extinguish or stifle. But if I ignore His voice, He often grows silent for a time, allowing me to feel the full weight of the consequences of my sinful choices.

There is no darker night of the soul than when God's Spirit grows silent. The hush echoes with an emptiness that nothing else can fill; a loneliness that no other relationship can satisfy.

Without Him there is no freedom, no peace, no joy, and no power to live a holy life. Does He live in you?

Test everything. Hold on to the good. Avoid every kind of evil. May God Himself, the God of peace, sanctify you through and through. May your whole spirit, soul, and body be kept blameless at the coming of our Lord Jesus Christ. The One who calls you is faithful and He will do it. (1 Thessalonians 5:21-24)

Praise be to the God and Father of our Lord Jesus Christ, who has blessed us in the heavenly realms with every spiritual blessing in Christ. For He chose us in Him before the creation of the world to be holy and blameless in His sight. (Ephesians 1:3-4)

Named for the Empress Maria Theresa, Theresienstadt was a military fortress that was built in the late 18th Century. It was located in what is now the Czech Republic near the convergence of the Ohre and Elba Rivers. The fort was surrounded by trenches which could be flooded, making it an ideal location for a military fort or a prison.

The fortress had housed prisoners during the late 19th Century, and was used as a political prison during World War I. After World War I, the area became part of the newly formed Czechoslovakia, in an area the Germans called Sudetenland. Hitler used the fact that the Sudetenland population was mainly of German ethnicity, to justify its annexation, and the subsequent weakening of Czechoslovakia in his subjugation of Eastern Europe.

As news of the Holocaust began to leak out, the Red Cross insisted on inspecting the "concentration camps" to determine for themselves whether the reports of atrocities were true. The Nazis decided to show them Theresienstadt, which was not an extermination camp, but was used as a ghetto/detention camp for prisoners who were on their way to Auschwitz and other death camps. Conditions were appalling. Starvation, overcrowding, and disease were rampant. Of the 150,000 prisoners who passed through, only 17,247 survived the war.

In preparing for the Red Cross visitors, the first order of Nazi business was to send several thousand prisoners to Auschwitz to be killed, thereby making the camp appear less crowded - and so that the stench coming from the crematorium would not belie the fraud.

Buildings were staged as shops, banks, a theater, and even a school for the children to attend (although it was actually illegal to teach a Jewish child under Nazi occupation). The children who were imprisoned there at the time were even forced to provide musical theater to entertain the inspectors. It may have been the last hours of normalcy in their short lives. Of course, it was all illusion.

Although the Nazis passed the Red Cross inspection, the reality of the horrors of the camp were unchanged. A coat of paint, curtains, deceptive signage, and some window boxes did not remove the stench of death and disease. Of more than 15,000 children who entered the gates of Theresienstadt, only about 100 survived to tell about it.

There are many Theresienstadt Churches around today. They meet in beautiful buildings, keep busy with activities and programs, and are full of Theresienstadt Christians who are dead and decaying in sin. They seem to be covered with the righteousness of Christ, but are trapped in the sin of Adam. They pass the world's inspection, but it is all an illusion. They live lives of pain and defeat, unwilling to surrender to the Sovereignty of God.

Sitting right down front each Sunday morning, they raise their hands during the praise choruses, feast on a sermon of "feel-good" Gospel, serve as Deacons or Elders, and teach a Bible Study or a Sunday School class. They spend their lives in search of "happiness", while never experiencing the peace and joy that come only through submission to the will of Christ. And of the thousands who enter the doors of those churches, not all will survive to enjoy eternity.

But for those who humble themselves and honestly seek Him, God has prepared a taste of Heaven on earth. The spiritual blessings that He pours into His children, the presence and work of His Spirit in our lives are but a foretaste of eternity in His presence.

At the moment of our salvation God placed us "in Christ", covered us with His righteousness, gave us a share in His inheritance, and made us a display of His character.

...just as the result of one trespass was condemnation for all men, so also the result of one act of righteousness was justification that brings life for all men. For just as through the disobedience of the one man (Adam) the many were made sinners, so also through the obedience of one Man (Jesus) the many will be made righteous. (Romans 5:18, 19).

Either we live "in Adam" or we live "in Christ". Either we are condemned or we are justified, cursed or blessed. It is our choice, and a choice that we can't avoid. Failure to choose Christ, is to choose Adam.

God sees the heart, not the illusion. We can wear a façade of righteousness, and even pass the inspection of the people in the community, but God sees the disease and decay that lies beneath.

It doesn't have to be that way. God's grace has provided a way out of the emptiness that marks the life of those who do not know Him. His Word is clear, *All have sinned. (Romans 3:23) The wages of sin is death but the free gift of God is eternal life. (Romans 6:23). If you confess with your mouth, 'Jesus is Lord', and believe in your heart that God raised Him from the dead you will be saved (Romans 10:9).*

From that time on Jesus began to preach, "Repent, for the kingdom of heaven is near". (Matthew 4:17)

Salvation comes through a God-given faith that is rooted in repentance and penetrates the depths of the soul, making all things new. Repentance from the belief that we are sovereign over our lives leads to faith in Christ. If we do not trust Christ's sacrificial death as the only remedy for our sin, we do not trust Him at all. That is why He came. It was God's plan and purpose for the life of the incarnate Christ.

There is a delicate synergy in the Gospel of Jesus Christ, balancing righteous judgment against redeeming grace on the fulcrum of divine mercy. Grace without judgment has no value. Judgment without grace leaves no hope. Grace without mercy is impotent. Mercy without repentance is a myth.

Grace presented without mercy is a cheap, weak lie. It lacks power to bring either forgiveness of sin or change to the life of those who follow its rambling path. This cheap grace is open-minded, but equally open to lies or truth - whichever seems socially or politically correct at the moment. It comes as no surprise that the world has rejected the existence of both Heaven and Hell so as to simply live for today, blissfully reveling in their ignorance of the Truth.

Not only is sin rampant, it has become the norm. From the pulpit we hear half-truths such as: we should not fear God because He loves everybody the same, never judge others, I'm Okay-You're Okay, God is everywhere so His kingdom is in everyone and everything, etc. All of these statements contain some truth, but a half-truth is a whole lie. Such philosophies have fostered the belief that a God of grace would not allow suffering or evil on the earth, much less cast people into hell.

But God's Word paints a very different picture. We are told repeatedly that God abhors those who choose to reject Him in pursuit of willful sin. (Psalm 5:5, 11:5, Leviticus 20:23, Hosea 9:15, and John 3:36 to name a few). Matthew 10:28 tells us to fear the one who can destroy both soul and body in hell. We cannot, and should not try to judge another person's relationship with God. We cannot see into their hearts. But we are commanded to hold those who claim the name of Christ accountable to the truth of the Gospel.

It used to be popular to say that a church is a hospital for sinners, and that is certainly a big part of her work. But hospitals are rarely comfortable places to be. The disease in our bodies is assaulted with everything from poisons to surgeries in order to repair the damage of injury or destroy an offending microbe.

Yet, it is becoming all too common for church-goers to warm the pews of a church without ever having to confront the disease of sin that is destroying their very souls. The truth of the damnation that awaits those who reject Christ must be balanced with the life-giving grace that was purchased by the shed blood of Christ. When our fellow adoptees stray from God, we are told to lovingly confront them with the truth, not to disgrace them, but so that they might be restored to fellowship with God.

Only the condemned need grace; and only God can bestow grace. The truth is that there is only one way to approach God and that is through Jesus Christ. He laid down His life in payment for the sins of those who would follow Him. He rose from the dead, and ascended to sit on what will one day be a throne of judgment over those who reject Him.

God is love and He has already extended the ultimate in love by taking upon Himself the punishment for our sin. Grace did not come cheap. Salvation is free to us, but it cost God dearly. Unbelief is the only sin of which the Holy Spirit convicts the lost. Rejecting His offer of salvation is the one sin which God will not forgive - the one for which He will cast perpetrators into hell (justice).

Awareness of our vulnerability before God is frightening; but ignorance of that vulnerability is far more dangerous. Every knee will someday bow in submission to God's sovereignty. The question is whether it will happen before or after we step across that line that divides physical life from death. Those who reject grace will receive justice. They will have chosen Hell.

God, in the person of Jesus Christ, came and dwelt among us. He brought His kingdom to us so that we could be freed from the power of sin; and so that we could dwell eternally with Him, never having to taste the horrors of damnation. His Holy Spirit dwells only within those who have surrendered to the truth that, through the atoning blood of Jesus Christ, God has purchased the right to rule their lives.

Autonomous grace completely ignores the problem of sin and is constructed on the lie that a very tolerant God loves us too much to send anyone to hell. Amazing grace accounts for the problem of sin through the sacrificial death of Christ, and is rooted in the truth that *God so loved the world that He gave His one and only Son, that whoever believes in Him should not perish but have eternal life. (John 3:16).*

Autonomous grace leaves you on your own for salvation. Amazing grace leads you to Christ. It is a matter of life or death. Which will you choose?

As He went along, He saw a man blind from birth. His disciples asked Him, "Rabbi, who sinned, this man or his parents that he was born blind?"

"Neither this man nor his parents sinned," said Jesus, "but this happened so that the work of God might be displayed in his life. As long as it is day, we must do the work of Him who sent Me. Night is coming, when no one can work. While I am in the world, I am the light of the world."

Having said this, He spit on the ground, made some mud with the saliva, and put it on the man's eyes. "Go" He told him, "wash in the Pool of Siloam" (this word means Sent). So the man went and washed, and came home seeing. (John 9:1-7)

I grew up in the era when John Wayne was a big star and westerns were among the most popular movies and television series in the United States, and likely many other countries around the world. They often depicted two cowboys having some kind of confrontation or negotiation at the bar in the local saloon. Agreement (or disagreement) would be reached, and one of them would say something like, "Here's mud in your eye". They would both down a shot of whiskey in one gulp and go their separate ways. Within context, they hardly seemed like words of hope.

But almost two millennia before television was dreamed possible, Jesus encountered a man who had never experienced light - only darkness. The disciples, equally blind in many ways, saw him only through a lens of cultural bias that said all misfortune was the result of sin. Despite having seen Jesus perform miracles, they failed to see that every encounter with Jesus is miraculous. Perhaps the disciples had lost the wonder of the miraculous. But for the blind man, the muddy miracle likely fulfilled the hopes of a lifetime.

It is easy to lose sight of the wonder of a God who humbled Himself to draw near His creation. The birth of a baby in a manger, who proved through signs and miracles that He is God, who stood in the gap between His creation and our self-ordained damnation, who carried the weight of our sins to the cross, is an amazing reality. It should bring us to our knees in awe and cause tears of unmerited joy each time the reality of His love floods our souls anew.

I don't know where you are, or what may be happening in your life right now. But I know that the Savior who made mud from His saliva and the dirt beneath a blind man's feet, still opens eyes and works miracles. He does not care about your past. He loves you and He can use even the dirt from your past to bring light for your future.

The problem with Christianity
is not that it has been tried and
found wanting, but that it has
been found difficult and left
untried.

- G. K. Chesterton

Part Six

Trust and obey,
For there's no other way
To be happy in Jesus,
But to trust and obey.

Be still and know that I Am God. (Psalm 46:10)

ach time I read from the first chapter of the Gospel of Luke, I am struck again by the contrast between Zechariah's and Mary's responses to seemingly impossible news. They were both frightened; and both questioned the Angel Gabriel, the messenger who was sent to each of them roughly six months apart. On the surface their questions appear quite similar, but there were subtle yet profound differences between the two.

Zechariah, a Hebrew priest in Jerusalem, was serving his rotation of "active duty". He had been chosen to enter the temple of God to burn incense during a time of assembled prayer. As he went about his priestly duties, Gabriel suddenly appeared beside the altar of incense, terrifying Zechariah. I doubt that any of us would be any less frightened by someone suddenly appearing before us, seemingly out of nowhere.

Gabriel's message to Zechariah was *Do not be afraid, Zechariah; your prayer has been heard. Your wife Elizabeth will bear you a son, and you are to give him the name John. He will be a delight to you, and many will rejoice because of his birth, for he will be great in the sight of the Lord. He is never to take wine or other fermented drink, and he will be filled with the Holy Spirit even from birth. Many of the people of Israel will he bring back to the Lord their God. And he will go on before the Lord, in the spirit and power of Elijah, to turn the hearts of the fathers to their children and the disobedient to the wisdom of the righteous--to make ready a people prepared for the Lord.* Certainly all good news!

The priest's question was, *How can I be sure of this? I am an old man and my wife is well along in years.* After praying for a son for so many years, Zechariah was already focused on the reasons why this could not happen. He wanted more assurance than the miraculous arrival of a messenger from God.

When I hear Gabriel's response in my mind's ear he sounds more than perturbed, almost indignant. The words are certainly a rebuke, *I am Gabriel, I stand in the presence of God, and I have been sent to speak to you and to tell you this good news. And now you will be silent and not able to speak until the day this happens, because you did not believe my words, which will come true at their proper time.*

To me it sounds like one of those "sit down and shut up" moments. In his silence, Zechariah would have the opportunity to watch and truly see the wonder of all that was unfolding in his life. As the next few months of his life played out, I expect he came to realize that it was actually a "be still and know" moment.

Meanwhile, Mary was a young girl living in the town of Nazareth in Galilee. The only things we really know about her is that she was a virgin and

156

she was engaged to marry Joseph. She was probably in her mid-teens and lived at home with her family when Gabriel was dispatched to speak to her.

She, too, was understandably troubled when the angel appeared and said, *Greetings you who are highly favored! The Lord is with you... Do not be afraid, Mary, you have found favor with God. You will be with child and give birth to a son, and you are to give him the name Jesus. He will be great and will be called the Son of the Most High. The Lord will give Him the throne of his father David, and He will reign over the house of Jacob forever; His kingdom will never end.*

Mary's response: *How will this be since I am a virgin?* Her question is superficially similar to Zechariah's question; but Mary was asking for clarification of the methods to be used. She was not questioning whether God was able to do what was being promised, as is illustrated in Gabriel's response: *The Holy Spirit will come upon you, and the power of the Most High will overshadow you. So the one to be born will be called the Son of God. Even Elizabeth, your cousin, is going to have a child in her old age, and she who was said to be barren is in her sixth month. For nothing is impossible with God.* To which Mary replied, *I am the Lord's servant, may it be to me as you have said.*

God is not offended by the question asked in faith. But He has little patience with those who question His Word, and by extension, His Character. He has nothing to prove to anyone. Yet He is infinitely gracious and often demonstrates His might or His mercy in such a way that reveals the unbound depth of His character, producing a faith-building exercise.

But, whether He demonstrates His miraculous power or, in His sovereignty, His answer to our sincerest questions is simply: Be still and know, He is trustworthy and can be trusted to do whatever is right and best.

And Jesus grew in wisdom and stature, and in favor with God and man. (Luke 2:52)

Whenever we think of Jesus, we usually picture a babe in a manger, or a man teaching, healing, confronting, and comforting, or a Suffering Savior hanging naked on a cross, with a footnote of an adolescent drilling the religious leaders in the Temple. But there was so much more to Him, to His life.

God sent Him here with a plan and a purpose. He came as a completely helpless infant and learned what it's like to be vulnerable and dependent on others. Before He preached a sermon on a hillside, he learned to say "Ema" and "Abba", Before He walked on water, He held tightly to His parents' hands and learned to walk on land.

Jesus grew just as we grow. He learned just as we learn. He grew to know God just as we learn to know Him. He was tempted just as we are tempted. But, each time He was tempted, He chose to take the "way out" that is promised in 1 Corinthians 10:13.

The Son who was given, was fully God; but the child who was born was just a man who was filled with the Spirit of God. Had he not fully experienced human life, He could not have been counted as having fulfilled the law with His perfect life, and become the perfect sacrifice for my sin.

Likewise, God's plan for me is to know Him. He is my destination and the vehicle by which I arrive. Because things have happened to me that I would not have chosen, or those that I foolishly did choose, does not disqualify me from fulfilling His purpose for me.

No one except Jesus Christ has ever lived out God's "Plan A" for his or her life. God's "Plan A" would be perfect, sinless, and holy with unbroken fellowship. But because we are sinners by nature, and He gave us freedom to choose, that doesn't happen.

The first rebellious moment, the moment when the heart begins to harden, becomes a detour on the path laid out for us. Jeremiah tells us: *The heart is deceitful above all things and beyond cure. (Jeremiah 17:9)*

God knows how we are. He remembers that He made us out of dust. We can neither surprise nor shock God. When we veer from the path He doesn't throw up His hands in horror and say, "Wow, I never saw that coming". Instead His Spirit brings conviction, sometimes a gentle nudge that brings us to the point of repentance and resets our course. Thus we begin again to grow in the grace and knowledge of our Lord and Savior, Jesus Christ. (2 Peter 3:18)

Our actions will never derail God's plans; He is bigger than anything that happens on earth. God has only one plan, one cure for the heart that is hardened by sin. His name is Jesus. He invades the sinful soul and performs a heart transplant: *And I will give you a new heart and put a new Spirit within you. I will remove your heart of stone and give you a heart of flesh. (Ezekiel 36:26) (HCSB)*

My detours may have altered the course, but not the destination of my life. I have not out-sinned God's grace. He loves me in spite of me. It is almost incomprehensible to me that He could take my stony, unworthy, crumbling heart and replace it with a heart that grows more open to Him each day. And bit by bit, He is reshaping this softer, moldable heart that He gave me, so that one day it will resemble His. Although the resemblance still may be slight, at least it has begun to change. He has a plan and He is accomplishing His plan for me to know Him, one heartbeat at a time.

The Lord is not slow in keeping His promise as some understand slowness. He is patient with you, not wanting anyone to perish, but everyone to come to repentance. But the day of the LORD will come like a thief. The heavens will disappear with a roar; the elements will be destroyed by fire, and the earth and everything in it will be laid bare.

Since everything will be destroyed in this way, what kind of people ought you to be? You ought to live holy and godly lives as you look forward to the day of God and speed its coming. (2 Peter 3:8-12)

*T*he worldwide trend toward laws banning so-called "hate speech" is leading to the criminalization of sharing the Truth of God's Word. We are asked to be tolerant of beliefs and practices with which we do not agree in the name of peace and harmony. And I whole-heartedly agree that on issues with no eternal significance, those which are not addressed by God's Word, we should all just get along. But when the Word, spoken by Jehovah, our Creator, is called hate speech the line must be drawn. We must choose carefully which hill we want to die on.

God is Love. He sacrificed all for the good of His creation. God is merciful beyond what we can imagine. But God is Holy. He alone is entitled to define right and wrong, good and evil. God does not have merely an opinion about such things; He made the rules and set them in stone. And while He is eternally patient with sinners, He is completely intolerant of deliberate sin. The biggest mistake we often make is to confuse tolerance with patience. To do so causes us to lose sight of our need for mercy; and mercy is never extended without repentance.

For the wages of sin is death; but the gift of God is eternal life in Christ Jesus. (Romans 6:23). ALL sin brings a death sentence. But God's love is so boundless that He would rather die for us than to give us over to our just punishment.

Without the shedding of blood there is no forgiveness of sin. (Hebrews 9:22). We must not make the mistake of believing that this verse is no longer true. ALL sin requires a blood sacrifice. That sacrifice which was paid for us by God through the death of His Son, Jesus Christ.

When we seek to compartmentalize our lives – professional life, love life, family life, social life, spiritual life, thought life, academic life, etc. – we deny our true purpose. Each of us is created to become a temple of God's Holy Spirit. When He comes to indwell us He provides focus and direction for our created purpose – life in Christ.

Do not put out the Spirit's fire; do not treat prophecies with contempt. Test everything. Hold on to the good. Avoid every kind of evil. (1 Thessalonians 5:19-22)

There is a growing trend among pastors and teachers who tread so lightly around the sensibilities of their congregants that they preach an empty, watered-down version of the Gospel. They teach a false god who is loving but not holy although it is God's holiness that makes His love reliable. Would not the faintest tolerance for sin in God's character refute the sacrifice of His Son?

If God could simply overlook sin, then no sacrifice would have been necessary. Once God had established perfection as His standard and identified what is sin, He would violate His own essence to lapse into apathy toward that which offends Him. To suggest that any facet of His nature might grow or shrink is to diminish Him. His steadfastness guarantees that He will not change His mind about you.

God loves you unconditionally, but He is completely intolerant of cherished sin in the hearts of His children. Once you truly belong to Him, He will root out the disobedience from your heart through the process of sanctification, whereby the dirty is made clean and the old is made new.

As Jesus said, "*Do not fear those who kill the body but are unable to kill the soul; but rather fear Him who is able to destroy both soul and body in hell." (Matthew 10:28)* If we're going to offend someone, better the people who sit on the pews than the Savior who died on a cross.

May God Himself, the God of peace, sanctify you through and through. May your whole spirit, soul and body be kept blameless at the coming of our Lord Jesus Christ. The One who calls you is faithful and He will do it. (1 Thessalonians 5:25-27)

Blessed is the man who does not walk in the counsel of the wicked or stand in the way of sinners or sit in the seat of mockers. But his delight is in the law of the Lord, and on His law he meditates day and night. He is like a tree planted by streams of water, which yields its fruit in season and whose leaf does not wither. Whatever he does prospers. (Psalm 1)

A favorite phrase of most toddlers is: "I can do it myself!" I don't know how many times I've heard that in the last 39 years. Sometimes it was funny watching my boys trying to master a new skill; but sometimes it was frustrating, and occasionally painful. There are times when parents can see the pitfalls and pratfalls that lie ahead but must let our children suffer consequences in order for them to learn the hard lessons.

When we fail to seek God's direction, we often find ourselves sinking in a quagmire of sin, addictions, broken relationships unplanned pregnancy, etc. God sees the future as clearly as He sees the past – and the hearts and minds of His creations. He loves you and wants to bless you beyond anything that you can imagine.

To believe that you can make better decisions without God than you can with Him is the same as saying that you are as smart as, or even smarter than Almighty God who made you. That's the same attitude of rebellion that got Lucifer kicked out of Heaven and Adam kicked out of Eden.

When you accept God's gift of salvation, you open a door that gives you access to the very heart of God; and you close off the enemy's access to your heart. God is ready, willing, and able to bless every area of your life. But what He cares most about is the condition of your heart, and your relationship with Him.

He paid the ultimate price for your heart. Jesus left glory, power, and honor to become a man – a sacrifice for His creation. He didn't die just once; He died to human desire each one of His roughly twelve thousand days on Earth. Each time He was tempted by the lure of sin, He turned to God's Word and to prayer for the wisdom and strength to overcome.

Then, one day He allowed Himself to be stripped naked, spat upon, tortured, publicly humiliated, and murdered in the most ghastly manner the Romans could imagine, just for you. If you were the only one who would ever need a savior, He still would have done it. He bought your eternal salvation and forgiveness for every sin, even rebellion.

If He needed to study the scriptures and pray, to seek God's guidance, what makes us think that we don't? Please don't just skim over this, let it penetrate your heart. To have experienced God's grace, to know the truth and take it lightly is to have a blasphemous heart.

The thing that God has shown me in my own life is that when I decide to do things my way, I close the door to God's blessing; and I give the enemy access to my life.

Satan is real and he is the only enemy that believers have. He comes to steal, kill, and destroy. He steals possessions, kills relationships, and destroys hope for the future. He wants to destroy your family's future. You never go into the wilderness alone, your family always goes with you. How much more of God's blessing on your life are you going to allow the enemy to steal?

God cannot fail, if He is the author of any venture, it will succeed. If Jesus had played golf, His score would have been 18 every time. If He opens a business, it will succeed. And everything that He directs His children to do is guaranteed and underwritten 100% to succeed and prosper unless there is greater profit in the humility learned through failure.

God's promise is that if you repent, turn back to Him, and submit to His lordship, He'll provide everything you need to fulfill His purpose for you. He'll lead you to places where you will find success, influence, and prosperity. Of course, His definition of prosperity is always revealed first in the spiritual realm; He cares more about your heart than your bank account.

If you earnestly seek Him, get to know Him, and grow to love Him, He will lift you out of whatever pit you're in and set your feet on solid ground. He will open the windows of Heaven and pour out a blessing too great for you to contain and it will overflow to bless everyone around you.

The generational curse lasts 3 or 4 generations, but the Bible says that the blessing poured out on those who turn to God lasts to 1000 generations. That's what I desperately want for my grandchildren and their grandchildren and their grandchildren, and so on for a thousand generations.

Our world today, even within the church, is really big on "free will". But once you have made the choice to become a child of God, you no longer have free will. You are either an obedient child or a disobedient child. God never gives His children up for adoption and when the prodigal returns, he rushes out to meet him with open arms.

He can and will fix every broken area of your life, if you will ask. Perhaps You have not because you ask not.

When the men came to Jesus, they said, "John the Baptist sent us to you to ask, 'Are you the one who is to come, or should we expect someone else?'"

At that very time Jesus cured many who had diseases, sicknesses and evil spirits, and gave sight to many who were blind. So he replied to the messengers, "Go back and report to John what you have seen and heard: The blind receive sight, the lame walk, those who have leprosy are cleansed, the deaf hear, the dead are raised, and the good news is proclaimed to the poor. Blessed is anyone who does not stumble on account of me." (Luke 7:18-23)

Skeptics point to variations in accounts of events portrayed in the Gospels as evidence that the Bible is somehow flawed. But, to me the differences make the accounts all the more believable. Had the four Gospels recorded exactly the same details about exactly the same events, three of them would have been unnecessary and a conspiracy would have been almost a certainty. It's the personal viewpoint expressed by each writer that reveals its honesty.

Each of the eyewitnesses to the ministry of Jesus Christ probably shared those moments that had the greatest personal impact on him. For more than a thousand days they followed Jesus around watching Him do the impossible, defy the laws of nature - turn the world on its head. Did the miraculous ever become commonplace to them? Did they ever, even for a moment, miss the wonder of what they were seeing?

Even with the written Word, we apparently know only the tip of the iceberg. The Apostle John tells us, *And there are also many other things that Jesus did, which, if they were written one by one, I suppose not even the world itself could contain the books that would be written. (John 21:25)*

The miracles performed by Christ were His calling cards, the introduction of God into the backdrop of history. They proclaim His Deity even as He stands knocking at the door of the sinner's heart. Not wanting the questions of those who earnestly seek Him to become stumbling blocks, He lived His incarnate life so as to remove all doubt about His identity.

He wants us to come to Him in confidence that He is stronger than our sins, deeper than our hurts, bigger than our needs, healer of our diseases, peace for our fears, corrector of our mistakes, bearer of our guilt, and Lord of our eternity.

He who made the blind to see still opens the eyes of lost and hurting people. The storms of this world still obey His voice. He who took a handful of clay and made man, still takes the ashes of our broken hopes and dreams and shapes them into lives of beauty and joy.

Every miracle that Jesus performed while He walked the dusty streets and trails of Judea had a dual purpose. He ministered healing to the hurting person in front of Him at that moment in time, but He also looked down through time and whispered to all who would come after, "See. I AM; I can fix that if you will let me." He does not want us to spend our lives dragging around the guilt and shattered dreams of the past. He wants them. All of them. He already knows everything each of us has ever done. He can't be shocked or disappointed.

He is the solution to every problem, the answer to every question, the sacrifice that gives value to every life. He never promised us a life free of problems; He did promise to never leave us alone in the midst of them. And so He spent His days showing us exactly what He is capable of doing with but a tiny seed of faith.

He wants to see His beloved set free from the power of sin, the trials of this world, and the discouragement of an uncertain future. He is the Way, the Truth, and the Life - grace for yesterday, strength for today, and hope for tomorrow.

Jesus performed many other signs in the presence of his disciples, which are not recorded in this book. But these are written that you may believe that Jesus is the Messiah, the Son of God, and that by believing you may have life in his name. (John 20:30-31)

All the Lord's ways show faithful love and truth to those who keep His covenant and decrees. (Psalm 25:10, HCSB)

Doubt is caustic. It eats away at faith and lays open a heart filled with fear, pain, anger, worry, confusion, discouragement, and regret. It eventually leaves you feeling alone and hopeless.

The Apostle Thomas has been much vilified through the centuries as "The Doubter". I think his doubt was the natural result of wrong perspective. He was focused on the last three days rather than the preceding three years. He saw Jesus perform miracles that must have truly stunned him at first. Had Thomas become too accustomed to the wondrous? Had the miraculous become so mundane that when the horrific cataclysm of the crucifixion interrupted the growing excitement of Jesus' rise to fame, he forgot the promises made so recently? Jesus had told the Twelve that He would die and that after three days He would rise.

Thomas had seen Jesus do everything that He said He could, and so much more. But in the shadow of the crucifixion, the news of Judas' betrayal and subsequent suicide, rumors that the authorities might be looking for the rest of them, Thomas quickly lost sight of the proven power and character of Christ. He must have isolated himself from the rest because it was the evening of the first day when Jesus appeared to them. I often wonder where he was... perhaps locked away somewhere alone and quivering at the sound of every footstep outside his door? Where was he early that morning when Mary knocked on the door to share the news of Jesus' greatest miracle?

I understand much of what Thomas was probably feeling. I've seen loved ones betrayed and murdered. I know the mind-numbing anguish that leaves your knees too weak to support your body weight. I know the confusion that leaves you unable to make casual conversation (sometimes for weeks or even months) and causes dread at the prospect of being with other people. And I know that it is in the darkest days that we most need the company of those who also know.

But I have something that Thomas didn't have. He wasn't there when Jesus breathed His Spirit into the other Apostles. He missed the greatest blessing of all, the Comforter. At the moment when the knees go weak, He stands you up and packs a bag that you don't know you will need. And with His arm wrapped tenderly around you He walks you through doors and days you never wanted to face. He holds the pieces of your shattered heart safely in His hand while He carefully and methodically walks you through the process of healing until one day you realize that you are scarred, but nonetheless whole.

I think the remedy for doubt is not so much belief as surrender. I believe a lot of things that are true and likely some that are not. My beliefs are irrelevant to my life until I act on them. When that moment of crisis came my heart's cry was "I can't do this, Lord. Please help me". I'm not sure if I even fully formed it as a thought. It was more a prayer of desperation flowing from the depths of my soul -- a moment of complete surrender.

A week after he became "Doubting Thomas" came a moment of surrender when Thomas saw the marks of crucifixion on Christ's body and cried out, "My Lord and my God". The reality of Christ's resurrection and victory over death changed Thomas' entire perspective on life, death, eternity, and the unlimited power of God. His was a declaration of both the truth of Christ's identity as the living God and Thomas' surrender to that Lordship.

Other early writings support the change in Thomas' perspective revealing that he went on to become a missionary to India, and possibly Iraq, Iran, and Syria. He likely was martyred around AD 72 in the Madras area of India -- pierced with a spear.

The cure for doubt remains the same for us as it was for Thomas. Focus on the resurrected Christ rather than the circumstances and momentary trials of this life. He is LORD whether we surrender or not; but to those who do surrender, He shows His unwavering faithfulness and love.

Yet I hold this against you: You have forsaken the love you had at first. Consider how far you have fallen! Repent and do the things you did at first. (Revelation 2:4-5)

I first met Christ as a 9-year-old child. I had been in church all my life and I certainly knew all about Him; but I did not get to know Him until I first came face to face with my own sinful condition. I never understood my need for a Savior until I grasped the hopelessness of trying to get to Heaven on my own.

My grandmother had just died, and for the first time in my life I faced the reality that death eventually comes to all of us. The concept of eternity was as new as it was frightening, and seemed like something that I should try to figure out. But I had no idea what to think about it, much less what to do.

Then one night at GA Camp, I learned that I did not have to figure it out after all. Everything had been done for me. A Savior had stepped out of eternity and entered the reality of my little world. He took my punishment; He died in my place, making it possible for me to become part of God's family.

Children are so unassuming. They trust just as they love: wide-open, enthusiastically, joyfully, and unconditionally. There is nobody as loving or as trusting as a child who has never know the pain of rejection or abuse. They run at first sight of you and jump into your arms for hugs. They bring every hurt and problem to you with tear-filled eyes. They curl up in your lap when they get scared or just need a place to rest.

This is the child-like faith and love that Jesus spoke of in Mark 10 when He said, *"Let the little children come to me, and do not hinder them, for the kingdom of God belongs to such as these."* I think God probably designed children as He did to demonstrate the relationship that He wants with us.

But as our head-knowledge grows, we often lose some of the child-like joy of knowing Christ. The distractions of life begin to dampen the intensity of our desire to be with Him. We battle our fears, try to provide for our own needs, suffer under the weight of pain and discouragement as though He did not exist; and we grow increasingly weary.

In our feelings-driven society it's easy to become self-centered, consumed with the allure of immediate gratification, and dependent on the government, the credit card company, or other people to provide for our needs - be they physical, material or emotional.

But God's plan is that we will be totally dependent on His provision for everything from the most basic physical needs to career and relationship counselling, health, and comfort on the hardest days.

God wants a relationship with us that brings such joy and satisfaction that we need nothing from human relationships, but are able to allow His love to flow through us and bless those around us. He provides all that we need so that we can then provide for the needs of others.

That kind of relationship does not just happen. If we fail to spend time with Him each day, our faith begins to look like a "Cliff-notes" version of the faith of the Bible. We hit the high points, gleaned from some sermon or self-help book. Meanwhile, we have exchanged the rich fabric of faith for a religious experience that often leaves Christ out of everything except for the sign on the door.

Sometimes we have to take a few steps back before we can go forward. I think it is time for the followers of Christ to begin to act like His children. It is time to open our Bibles and our hearts so that our Heavenly Father can reignite the fires of passionate love from the fading embers of our faith - no matter how deep they may be buried in the ashes of sin, rebellion, or apathy. He is waiting with open arms and a lap that's big enough to hold all of us.

Because of the increase of wickedness, the love of most will grow cold, but he who stands firm to the end will be saved. And this gospel of the kingdom will be preached in the whole world as a testimony to all nations, and then the end will come. (Matthew 24:12-14).

As for you, you were dead in your transgressions and sins, in which you used to live when you followed the ways of this world and of the ruler of the kingdom of the air, the spirit who is now at work in those who are disobedient. All of us also lived among them at one time, gratifying the cravings of our flesh and following its desires and thoughts. Like the rest, we were by nature deserving of wrath. But because of His great love for us, God, who is rich in mercy, made us alive with Christ even when we were dead in transgressions - it is by grace you have been saved. (Ephesians 2:1-5)

There is a vast difference between the "Laws of Moses" and the Law of God. Moses was given a set of laws, rules, and guidelines that I believe were necessary if the Israelites were to survive their time of wandering in the wilderness. Proper hygiene and sanitation were essential to prevent pandemic disease within the massive mobile refugee camp that was the nation of Israel. Many of those taboos were lifted directly when God spoke to Peter in a dream, as described in Acts 10.

Conversely, the Law of God is absolute and transcendent. God doesn't change with the times and; neither does His law. When Jesus said, If you love me, keep my commands, I believe He was speaking as Creator as much as Savior. He and the Father are one; Jesus is the Law-Giver, just as His Father is the Law-Giver. As God, Jesus gave the Law. As the sinless Savior, Jesus fulfilled the Law. As the Judge Advocate, Jesus both prosecutes unbelievers and intercedes for His own. We show our love for Him by keeping His commands or Laws. When Jesus died, the Temple curtain was ripped open signifying the open relationship between God and man which no longer requires any mediator except Jesus Christ.

God's law also enables us to reclaim the joy that too often gets lost in the pursuit of happiness. It shows us how to live in intimacy with God and in harmony with other people. The Law of God exists for our protection. One needs only to look around at the chaotic condition of this world to understand the damage that is done when God's law is ignored.

Just as we live under Grace because of the perfect sacrifice of Jesus Christ, every time the God of the Old Testament accepted an offering or sacrifice it was an act of grace on His part. Were those offerings simply hints of the sacrifice of Christ? Was it not the blood of Christ that made prior sacrifices acceptable to God?

Any other offering is merely the returning of borrowed goods to the Creator of the offering. Only the sacrifice of one who is both eternal and uncreated could be precious enough to bridge the chasm created between God and man when Adam sinned. God is that Holy; Sin is that egregious.

As Isaiah said, *All of us have become like one who is unclean, and all our righteous acts are like filthy rags; we all shrivel up like a leaf, and like the wind our sins sweep us away. (Isaiah 64:6)*

The Word makes it clear that God cares as much about the condition of my heart as He does about my outward behavior. He looks deeply into the soul and determines motivation. This is where He does His work of regeneration in the life of a believer. He isn't interested in obedience that is an attempt to manipulate Him or impress other people. He looks for the heart that is surrendered to His Lordship and filled with His Spirit.

The acts of the flesh are obvious: sexual immorality, impurity and debauchery; idolatry and witchcraft; hatred, discord, jealousy, fits of rage, selfish ambition, dissensions, factions and envy; drunkenness, orgies, and the like. I warn you, as I did before, that those who live like this will not inherit the kingdom of God.

But the fruit of the Spirit is love, joy, peace, forbearance, kindness, goodness, faithfulness, gentleness and self-control. Against such things there is no law. Those who belong to Christ Jesus have crucified the flesh with its passions and desires. Since we live by the Spirit, let us keep in step with the Spirit. Let us not become conceited, provoking and envying each other. (Galatians 5:19-26)

Now faith is confidence in what we hope for and assurance about what we do not see. This is what the ancients were commended for. By faith we understand that the universe was formed at God's command, so that what is seen was not made out of what is visible. By faith Abel... By faith Enoch... By faith Noah... By faith Abraham, Isaac, Jacob, Sarah, Joseph, Moses, Rahab, Gideon, David, Samuel... These were all commended for their faith though none of them received what had been promised, since God had planned something better for us so that only together with us would they be made perfect. (Hebrews 11) (Selected)

Therefore, since we are surrounded by such a great cloud of witnesses, let us throw off everything that hinders and the sin that so easily entangles. And let us run with perseverance the race marked out before us, fixing our eyes on Jesus the pioneer and perfecter of our faith For the joy set before Him He endured the cross, scorning its shame, and sat down at the right hand of the throne of God. Consider Him who endured such opposition from sinners so that you will not grow weary and lose heart. (Hebrews 12:1-3)

The eleventh chapter of Hebrews is a litany of faith in Christ, even though all of the people listed there had died (or like Enoch been taken up alive) long before the angels delivered tidings of great joy to frightened shepherds in the countryside near Bethlehem. It was no less humble awareness of their total dependence on God's provision that was credited to them as righteousness before God.

While each story is different, each individual displayed his or her faith by living out God's unique plan through obedience to His leadership and direction. They pressed on regardless of the path those around them took, and despite the jeers and taunts of the ones who watched their stories unfold. I can only imagine the abuse Noah and his sons endured during the hundred years they labored on a giant boat when no one had as yet even seen it rain. Or the obscenities shouted at the Israelites from atop the soon to crumble walls of Jericho, but they pressed on.

Faith is always demonstrated through action. Perhaps the greatest demonstration of faith in action was played out on Mount Moriah when Abraham trudged to the top with Isaac, a load of firewood, and what must have been a very heavy heart. Yet his final words to his servants spoke volumes about the depth of his faith, He said to his servants, *"Stay here with the donkey while I and the boy go over there. We will worship and then we will come back to you." (Genesis 22:5)*

Abraham never doubted that his son would be coming back down the mountain with him. He likely wondered whether God would provide another sacrifice or simply raise Isaac from the dead after he was sacrificed.

But Abraham believed the promises that God had spoken to him; and against his natural instincts, he obeyed God. The nation of Israel stands today, as the Hebrew people have stood throughout history, in testimony to the faithfulness of God to keep His promises.

So when we are besieged by the devil's flaming arrows, we can cower in fear, we can stand there whining about our problems, or we can plant our feet and raise our shield of faith reminding ourselves that Satan is, and always has been, a liar.

Just knowing that my redemption through the shed blood of Jesus Christ has crushed the enemy's right to taunt me is not enough. It isn't really faith unless I act on what I know by obeying God's instructions. When God calls my name, I must step forward and obey.

So faith comes from what is heard, and what is heard comes through the message about Christ. (Romans 10:17)

If any of you lacks wisdom, he should ask God, Who gives generously to all without finding fault, and it will be given to him. (James 1:5)

*T*here are some prayers that God will always answer with a resounding "Yes". One is certainly a sincere request to know Him better; another is for wisdom. There are many who exemplify human wisdom; but I Corinthians 1:24 says, "...the foolishness of God is wiser than man's wisdom...". And if there is anything this world needs right now it is a healthy dose of God's wisdom.

Intellect and common sense have been proven wholly inadequate for understanding the existence of the Good and evil which have directed the course of human history. One example of this innate inadequacy is Christopher Hitchens, a brilliant author and philosopher, as well as, staunch humanist and atheist. His intellect made him a provocative debater, taking on liberal and conservative alike.

There was a well-reasoned consistency to his philosophy that was impervious to the winds of societal acceptability. As he matured, his political leanings moved from radically liberal to fairly conservative. He believed whatever he wanted and did not care what others thought.

He believed life begins at conception, was a staunch supporter of George W. Bush, and the wars in Afghanistan and Iraq. He was a critic of Bill Clinton and his White House sexual escapades and flagrant perjuries, publishing No One Left To Lie To while the rest of the left circled their wagons around Clinton. His world-view was formed of a peculiar combination of common sense, intellectualism, and a healthy dose of denial. He had an opinion about everything and readily shared his opinions.

He was, by human standards, a brilliant man; yet by biblical standards, he was a fool. That seems like a harsh statement, but Psalm 14:1 says, *The fool says in his heart, 'There is no God'*. According to his obituary, Hitchens never repented of his beliefs. He never found peace with God.

He settled his destiny with his unyielding refusal to bow before his Creator. He denied the love and sacrificial gift of eternity that were so freely offered to him. Belief in God would have meant accountability to God. To paraphrase Isaiah:

He heard, but never understood; he saw but never perceived. His heart was callused, his ears dull, his eyes closed. Otherwise he might have seen with his eyes, heard with his ears, understood with his heart, and turned and been healed. From Isaiah 6:9-10

Widely prayed for, Hitchens apparently hardened his heart to the beckoning of the risen Savior who had suffered to secure an eternal home for him in Heaven. A home that will apparently sit empty for all eternity. I don't know exactly what God had planned for Hitchens' life, but I know that he could have done much to further the Kingdom of Heaven. By now he knows the folly of the life he chose.

Sadly, modern academia has been appropriated by those whose hearts are hard toward God. They indoctrinate the brightest young minds with the myth that science and faith are mutually exclusive. But a long line of scientific and mathematical geniuses from Sir Isaac Newton, to Blaise Pascal, Albert Einstein, and Dr. Francis Collins (Head of the Human Genome Project) would say otherwise. André-Marie Ampère (1775-1836), French physicist and founder of classical electromagnetism wrote:

The True Scientist

Happy the one who in his learned watches,
Contemplating the marvels of this vast universe,
Before so much beauty, before so much grandeur,
Bows the knee and acknowledges the divine creator.
I do not share the foolish incoherence
Of the scientist who would contest the existence of God,
Who would close his ears to what the heavens declare,
And refuse to see what shines before his eyes.
To know God, to love Him, to offer Him a pure homage
*That is true knowledge and the study of the wise.***

You don't have to be an intellectual giant to become wise; you need only to ask God. He is the master craftsman. He can replace the mind of a fool with the mind of Christ - filled with His wisdom, understanding, and Spirit.

How much better to get wisdom than gold, to choose understanding rather than silver. (*Proverbs 16:16*)

** Translation by Dr. Fredrick Skiff, used by permission

Charm is deceptive, and beauty is fleeting; but a woman who fears the LORD is to be praised. (Proverbs 31:30)

Then Shall Live, written by Gloria Gaither, is a beautiful lyric set to Jean Sibelius' haunting melody, *Finlandia*. Whenever I hear it I think of Mama. She loved. Can there be a greater epitaph than that? Mama had a very hard life filled with disappointment, hurt, and hard work, even when she was a child. But she loved.

She had an unhappy, sometimes harsh mother – but she loved. Grandma was a voluntary invalid which meant that Mama and her sister were taking turns attending school and running a household when they should have been in the fourth and sixth grades respectively. She was emptying bedpans, cooking, cleaning, and doing laundry for a family of nine when she should have been playing with dolls. Grandma could be verbally, and sometimes physically, abusive.

But Mama loved her mother and, after her father's death, along with some of her brothers and their wives, took care of her for more than 40 years – as long as Grandma lived. If she had any anger or hard feelings toward her mother, it never showed. And Mama became the mother that I guess she wished her mother had been.

She had a sometimes distant, quick-tempered husband, but she loved. Daddy had a kind heart, but years of shift-work made him irritable. His life also had been hard. The son of good, honest sharecroppers, who labored long for very little return, Daddy, like Mama, worked very hard from childhood on. As a paratrooper with the All American 82nd Airborne during World War II, he saw unspeakable things that I think left deep scars. My parents were both very generous with what they had. If they knew of anyone with a need that they could meet, it was quietly met, a quality I see carried on in my sons.

Mama was by no means perfect, but she was strong, gentle, loving and faithful. Many nieces and nephews remember Mama as joyful, fun, gentle, and funny. The day of her funeral some of my cousins shared what sweet memories they had of their trips to visit us in the summer. We were far from rich, but at times, some of our family had it even harder than we did.

Still, when any of our family came to stay, Mama cooked and baked cakes. Or she would pack a picnic, load everyone into whatever car we had at the time, and head to the beach. In the 50's and 60's cars were usually big and sturdy. And with no pesky seat belts (which you really did not need in those cars) you could squeeze a lot of kids into the back seat. But their favorite memory of Mama was the impromptu dance lesson one day in our kitchen when she taught us all how to do the Charleston.

When I asked Mama how she could love so faithfully those who had not always reciprocated, her response was earthshakingly simple, "Because God has loved me so much more than I deserve." She was eternally thankful for Christ's sacrifice on her behalf.

And there it is. So simple, yet so deep. She loved because she had come to understand the depth of God's love. She lived out her belief that love is a verb – and commitment is a choice. In order to stop loving the people around her, she must first stop loving God. To choose not to love would have been to turn her back on her Savior whom she loved most of all.

Mama believed, and taught her three daughters to believe, that choosing not to love is the same as saying that the price that Jesus paid just didn't matter. Her life had been hard, but she had suffered nothing compared to what Christ had suffered for her.

She wasn't trying to impress anyone. She was just hoping for the day when she would hear her Lord say, "Well done, good and faithful servant". I have no doubt that she heard it on April 26, 1992, when she left her earthly body to go to her eternal Home.

She never stopped being thankful, and her "attitude of gratitude" kept her eyes focused on the prize for which God had called her heavenward. She set the bar high, but I am striving to live up to it. I've made too many mistakes to come very close, *but I press on to take hold of that for which Christ Jesus took hold of me* – to become like Him, just as Mama did.

And each of the builders had his sword strapped at his side while he built. (Nehemiah 4:18)

The people of Israel were discouraged, afraid, endangered – living in the ruins of what once had been a great nation. Theirs had been a kingdom that epitomized wealth, power, and security. But, they grew proud of their accomplishments; and they lost sight of God. Adopting the ways of the surrounding nations, they began to worship other gods, even sacrificing their own children to the gods of decadence, lavish living and sexual promiscuity. And God had shown them what life is like without Him -- Captivity in Babylon.

After the Persians conquered the Babylonians the Israelites had been allowed to trickle back home. But those who returned found a very different land than they remembered. Jerusalem was in ruins, the laughingstock of her neighbors. There was no wealth, no power, and no food.

Meanwhile, Nehemiah had risen to a position of great trust in the court of Artaxerxes, King of Persia. As cup-bearer to the King, Nehemiah had gained the king's trust, and friendship. When news of conditions in Jerusalem reached him, Nehemiah was heartbroken and it showed. After spending time in fasting and repentance, he returned to serve the king.

When Artaxerxes learned the reason for his friend's grief, he sent Nehemiah home to Jerusalem with letters of safe passage, and orders of provision for the needed materials to rebuild the walls of Jerusalem.

Like ancient Jerusalem, the walls of our hearts, our homes, and our nations have crumbled around us. Truth has been marginalized in today's culture of tolerance. But God has not changed, nor can He be marginalized. He is God. He keeps the sun shining, the earth turning, gravity in place, and He holds the universe in perfect tension. He has entrusted His family with a vital message to share with a hardened world.

His message is the same today as it always was: Repent, for the Kingdom of God has come near. He demands that His Bride repent of her adulterous relationship with the world, so that her manner will match her message. We must rebuild the walls of faith that made this nation the beacon of hope that once lit the way for a hurting world.

God acts in response to His people. There have always been atheists, apostates, and pagans among us. They have no effect on God's decision-making. Despite the teaching of naysayers and revisionists, God built this nation on the faith of the Church.

And it is the Church that He is calling to repentance. It is the Church whose humble prayers of submission He will answer. On the eve of Sodom's destruction, it was for the sake of righteous men that God was willing to spare the city - had He been able to find any.

We can rebuild our nation as the Israelites rebuilt Jerusalem in Nehemiah's day by living authentically as followers of Christ. We must humble ourselves before Him, know Him, worship Him, and obey Him, working with sword in hand, just as the Israelites did. Our weapons are the helmet of Salvation, the shield of faith, and the Sword of the Spirit, which is the Word of God.

In sacrificing obedience to God's Word on the altar of tolerance, we have become complicit in the destruction of our own culture. Our lives often look no different from the lives of nonbelievers around us. We fail to mirror, even faintly, His perfect Holiness. There is little evidence of the obedience that He requires of those who would draw near to Him.

Make no mistake, those who refuse God's Grace, bought with the blood of Christ, will be judged according to God's Law – the relevance of which they now deny. When He says to them, Depart from me, I never knew you, they will finally understand the grave consequences of the choices that they made.

Are you not deceived because you don't know the Scriptures or the power of God? (Mark 12:24)

Once you were alienated from God and were enemies in your minds because of your evil behavior. But now he has reconciled you by Christ's physical body through death to present you holy in his sight, without blemish and free from accusation-- if you continue in your faith, established and firm, not moved from the hope held out in the gospel. This is the gospel that you heard and that has been proclaimed to every creature under heaven, and of which I, Paul, have become a servant. Now I rejoice in what was suffered for you, and I fill up in my flesh what is still lacking in regard to Christ's afflictions, for the sake of his body, which is the church. I have become its servant by the commission God gave me to present to you the word of God in its fullness--the mystery that has been kept hidden for ages and generations, but is now disclosed to the saints. To them God has chosen to make known among the Gentiles the glorious riches of this mystery, which is Christ in you, the hope of glory. We proclaim him, admonishing and teaching everyone with all wisdom, so that we may present everyone perfect in Christ. (Colossians 1:21-28)

Too many people go through life feeling they are of no real value to anyone. A young girl grows up believing that she is ugly or stupid because people told her she was. Requests for help in overcoming her inadequacies may have been met with derision. Perhaps even spiritual growth brought ridicule. Suffering from low self-esteem, she became a fearful person, gullible and an easy target for abusive people. Withdrawn from the world, she missed a lot of opportunities to share the joy of others.

Perhaps you know someone who is naturally shy, but even beyond that has a fear of being noticed. Even his posture droops inward. Preferring to blend into the background, it is very difficult for him to approach people that he does not know well because of his doubt that he will be accepted. He fears rejection.

He goes through life hunched over, burdened by the sense of shame and worthlessness he carries. He may be terrified of speaking in public. In short, He believes the lies that people have said about him, rather than looking to the One who made him to find the truth.

Everybody wants to be loved, respected, and appreciated. Those who become convinced that they are none of those things may set about hiding the "truth". They may find themselves feeling like impostors, even among their family and friends. I've heard it said that God never made anything that He couldn't fix. And I know from personal experience that it's true.

As we begin to open up to the Light of His love, we see a very different picture of our intrinsic value. We find that we have value simply because God made us in His image. His love gives us value.

Whatever virtues we have are sacred, inviolate gifts from God. If you dislike the physical attributes or spiritual gifts you have been given, you criticize God's judgment. What greater pride can there be than either to believe ourselves superior to others, or at the opposite end of the spectrum, to call God's workmanship somehow inferior.

We take God's wonderful gifts and believe ourselves to be brilliant if we manage to accomplish anything at all with them. Pride takes many forms and has many consequences. Believing I am the "most" anything is pride. It runs the gamut of thinking you are superior because of some accomplishment, to being afraid to attempt anything because of perceived inadequacies. One is as devastating as the other. Both are rooted in being too "self" focused.

All glory and honor ultimately belong to God, because apart from Him we are worthless. If you are a good athlete, He gave you the skill and co-ordination. If you are a musician, He gave you the voice, the ear, and the talent to use them. If you are a rocket scientist, He gave you the intellect and logic to understand the Physics of flight. Whatever you are capable of accomplishing is because of the way He "knit you together". And whatever He gifted you to do, He will empower you to accomplish. If you are proud or ashamed of those abilities, you dishonor Him. If you pretend they don't exist, you deny Him.

The god of this age has blinded the minds of unbelievers, so that they cannot see the light of the gospel of the glory of Christ, who is the image of God. For we do not preach ourselves, but Jesus Christ as Lord, and ourselves as your servants for Jesus' sake. For God, who said, "Let light shine out of darkness," made his light shine in our hearts to give us the light of the knowledge of the glory of God in the face of Christ. But we have this treasure in jars of clay to show that this all-surpassing power is from God and not from us. We are hard pressed on every side, but not crushed; perplexed, but not in despair; persecuted, but not abandoned; struck down, but not destroyed. (2 Corinthians 4:4-9)

If you will trust Him and obey His leading, you can bring Him the honor and glory that He deserves. Each of us is created in His image, for the purpose of reflecting His love. The talent, the ability, the intellect, and the power to fulfill our purpose come from God. As more of Christ gets into you, more of your heart, your mind, and your ego will be focused on Him. As you become increasingly focused on His glory, you will come to understand who you are in Christ. Then you will find true fulfillment and happiness in Him. That is my goal: Christ in me, the hope of glory.

ABOUT THE AUTHOR

Vickie Rutland lives in rural Georgia with her husband Jimmy, their cat, Mama Yard Cat (that's what happens when you let an engineer take the cat to the vet before she has been named), and Lulu their Black Labrador grand-puppy. Vickie is the creator of two blogs with readers from fifty-four countries, on six continents. She is still waiting for a reader from Antarctica.

Made in the USA
Charleston, SC
17 October 2014